CONCISE NEEDLECRAFT

DATE	NAME	FORM	Issued by
12/1/82	M. CLARK	5⁶	PB
6/9/84	Beverly Rogers	4 PKM	PB

CONCISE NEEDLECRAFT

Olive Christensen

WHEATON

A Division of Pergamon Press

Illustrated by R. F. Summers

A. Wheaton & Company Limited (*A Division of Pergamon Press*) Hennock Road, Exeter EX2 8RP

Pergamon Press Ltd, Headington Hill Hall, Oxford OX3 0BW

Pergamon Press Inc., Maxwell House, Fairview Park, Elmsford, New York 10523

Pergamon of Canada Ltd, 75 The East Mall, Toronto, Ontario M8Z 2L9

Pergamon Press (Australia) Pty Ltd, 19a Boundary Street, Rushcutters Bay, N.S.W. 2011

Pergamon Press GmbH, 6242 Kronberg/Taunus, Pferdstrasse 1, Frankfurt-am-Main, Federal Republic of Germany

First edition 1977
Reprinted 1978

Printed in Great Britain by A. Wheaton & Co. Ltd, Exeter

ISBN 0 08 018306 9

CONTENTS

INTRODUCTION

Exploring the art of needlecraft has many rewards. Well-fitting clothes, made in your own choice of colour, quality and style, may be made at a minimal cost. A measure of skill must be achieved to give the desired results, but useful and attractive articles may be made by everyone once the basic skills have been mastered. This book is for all students who like to sew and wish to explore the art of needlecraft. It sets out all the necessary basic skills, clearly and concisely.

ABBREVIATIONS

S. of G.	*Straight of grain*
R.S.	*Right side*
W.S.	*Wrong side*
C.F.	*Centre front*
C.B.	*Centre back*
F.L.	*Fitting line*
Fig.	*Figure*

Chapter 1

EQUIPMENT

Good quality equipment is important for producing high quality work.

Workroom. Six essential items.
1. Large work table.
2. Full length mirror.
3. Sewing machine, preferably electric.
4. Hanging wardrobe and cupboard.
5. Drawers for storage.
6. Adjustable dressmaker's stand.

Pressing Equipment. Eight items.
1. Steam or dry iron.
2. Skirt board.
3. Sleeve board.
4. Padded roller.
5. Tailor's cushion.
6. Velvet board.
7. Pressing cloth.
8. Brush.

Personal Equipment. Seventeen items.
1. Needles: various sizes 1–12.
2. Pins (steel).
3. Tape measure 152 cm.
4. Thimble (metal).
5. Scissors: large—for cutting out.
6. Scissors: small—for embroidery.
7. Scissors: medium—for cutting paper.
8. Thread for tacking and sewing.
9. Stiletto for making eyelet holes.
10. Tailor's chalk for marking cloth.
11. Pinking shears.
12. 'Quick unpick'.
13. Bodkin for threading tape, elastic, etc.
14. Tracing wheel for marking.
15. Carbon paper for marking: special dressmaker's type.
16. Hem leveller.
17. Pin cushion.

Care of Equipment

Store all this equipment in a dry place, such as a drawer or large tool box, with divisions for easy access. The ironing equipment and sewing machine should also be stored in a dry place, preferably a purpose-built cupboard. The pressing cloths and ironing board covers need frequent laundering.

SEWING MACHINES

These can be semi- or fully automatic, hand-operated or electric.

Semi-automatic machines do straight stitching, zig-zag stitching and three or four fancy pattern stitches. Satin stitch, a close zig-zag, can be regulated (by the directions of the instruction manual) to produce buttonholes. Fully automatic machines do the same stitches as the semi-automatic, and in addition many fancy stitch patterns, and automatic buttonholes.

These machines when used with skill carry out many exciting and time-saving processes, such as embroidery, appliqué, mending and darning, tucking, and blind hemming. The most reputable machine manufacturers give good lessons and demonstrations, and it is wise to take full advantage of this service. The cheaper automatic machines on the market are an unwise buy.

The sewing machine should be cleaned and oiled frequently, following the manufacturer's instructions.

Using the Sewing Machine. Six Rules.

1. Learn the parts of the machine. (Fig. 1)
2. Thread as instructions direct.
3. Test all stitches on double material.
4. Watch machine foot edge when stitching, not the needle.
5. Keep bulk of work on your left.
6. Always remove work towards the back of the machine.

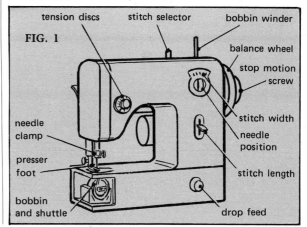

FIG. 1

tension discs stitch selector bobbin winder
balance wheel
stop motion
screw
stitch width
needle position
stitch length
needle clamp
presser foot
bobbin and shuttle
drop feed

Common Machine Faults in Use

1. Needle not threaded from the ridge side.
2. Cotton not between tension discs.
3. Tension too loose or tight.
4. Blunt needle.
5. Incorrect threading procedure.

NEEDLES AND THREADS
Needles.

Six Types	Uses
1. Sharps: medium length	General sewing
2. Betweens: short length	Fine work
3. Straws: long length	Tacking and millinery
4. Darning: long length	Darning
5. Crewel: medium length, long eye	Embroidery
6. Tapestry: long eye, blunt point	Canvas work

The higher the number the finer the needle.

Fabric Weight	Needle size
Heavy and thick	5–6
Medium	7–8
Fine and light	8–9
Synthetics	8–9
Beadwork	10–11

Sewing Threads

Cotton
Mercerized cotton
Pure silk
Synthetic thread
Linen thread
Buttonhole twist

Thread is sold in many thicknesses: 20 is a heavy thread for heavy work, 40 and 50 for dressmaking and average use; 100 is very fine.

The general rule is to use a thread corresponding to the fabric, and to choose a shade darker than the fabric rather than lighter. For finer fabric use finer thread.

Chapter 2

MEASUREMENTS AND PATTERNS

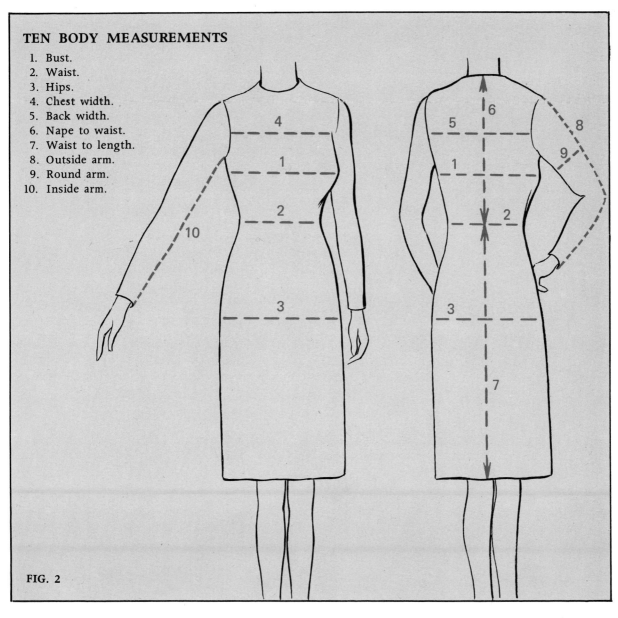

TEN BODY MEASUREMENTS

1. Bust.
2. Waist.
3. Hips.
4. Chest width.
5. Back width.
6. Nape to waist.
7. Waist to length.
8. Outside arm.
9. Round arm.
10. Inside arm.

FIG. 2

Bust.   Measure round fullest part with tape slightly raised at the back.

Waist. Measure round natural waistline comfortably.

Hips.   Measure round largest part.

Two fingers should be placed inside the tape measure, to allow for ease.

Take other measurements as in Fig. 2.

CHOICE OF PAPER PATTERN

Buy skirt and trouser patterns to your waist size, and dress, blouse, suit and coat patterns etc. to your bust size. If the correct size is unobtainable, get the next larger size. The pattern can then be adapted.

Table of pattern sizes in inches and centimetres.

Size	10		12		14		16		18	
	in	cm	in	cm	in	cm	in	cm	in	cm
Bust	$32\frac{1}{2}$	83	34	86	36	91	38	99	40	102
Waist	24	61	$25\frac{1}{2}$	65	27	68	29	74	31	79
Hips	$34\frac{1}{2}$	88	36	91	38	97	40	102	42	107

1. Select your pattern from well known and reliable makers, as these have better styles and instructions, and will therefore give better results more easily.

2. Notice where all seams, darts and fashion lines are, in relation to your figure shape and height. Simple lines well cut can often look smarter than too much drapery. The occasion for which the garment is required must also be considered.

3. Decide on a suitable fabric. Take into account its width, weight, cost and the amount required. If interfacing is needed, find the type, weight and amount. Zip fasteners, buttons and bindings may be needed, plus two reels of matching sewing thread. Particulars of these are on the back of each pattern envelope. Time is well spent in making a shopping list of your requirements.

USING THE PATTERN

Study the enclosed instruction sheet for the number of pattern pieces that will be required for the version you have chosen. Remove and put away the pieces not required. Then study the pattern symbols.

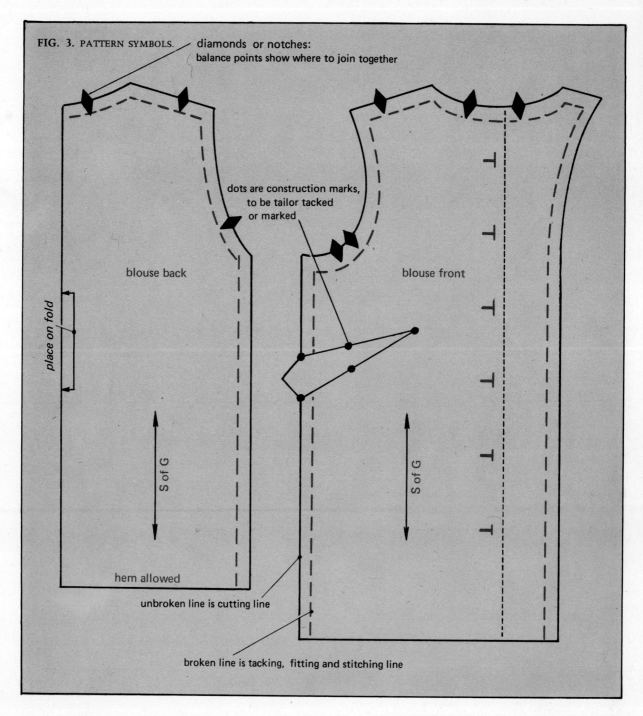

FIG. 3. PATTERN SYMBOLS.

diamonds or notches: balance points show where to join together

dots are construction marks, to be tailor tacked or marked

blouse back

blouse front

place on fold

S of G

S of G

hem allowed

unbroken line is cutting line

broken line is tacking, fitting and stitching line

ADAPTATION OF PATTERNS

Positions where alterations should be made: to shorten, lengthen and widen.

FIG. 4

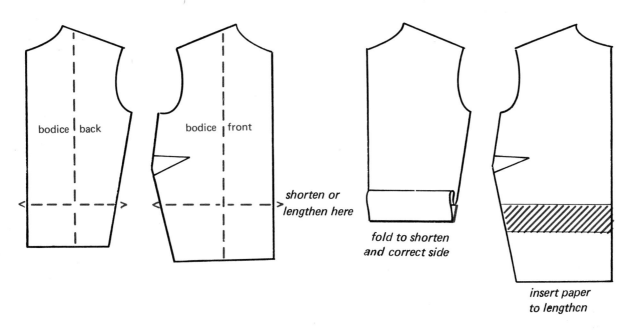

shorten or lengthen here

fold to shorten and correct side

insert paper to lengthen

FIG. 5

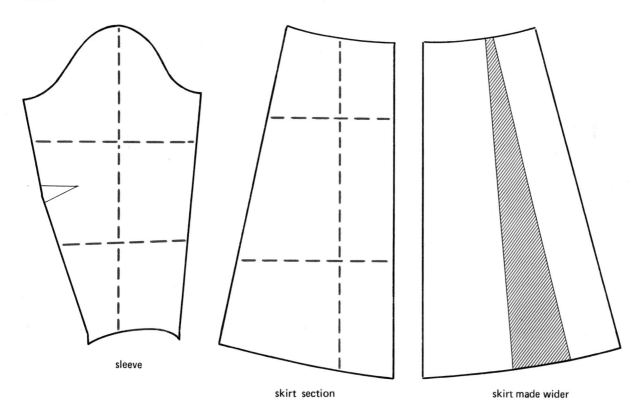

sleeve

skirt section

skirt made wider

Reminder: A fold of 4 cm double = 8 cm.

It is necessary to experiment with pattern adaptation. Care must always be taken to keep the balance of the design, so watch the spacing of darts, pockets and button positions. Shortening a flared skirt from the bottom edge makes it narrower.

Chapter 3

PREPARATION AND CUTTING OUT

FABRIC PREPARATION
Method

1. Test fabric for shrinkage as follows:
   Cut two pieces of fabric the same size. Wash one in hot water and press, and then compare with untreated piece. If the fabric has shrunk, then the whole length must be treated and shrunk before cutting out.
2. *Either* a) If the fabric is washable, dip into water without creasing it, then drip dry and press on wrong side if required.
   or b) Cover the fabric with a damp cloth and press

evenly all over. The above process is unsuitable for velvet or pile fabrics.

3. Check the grain; when the fabric is folded with edges together, it should lie flat. If it does not do so, pull the fabric firmly on the cross grain until it does.
4. Fabric with a nap i.e. velvet, facecloth, etc. or a one-way design, will require all the pattern pieces placed in the same direction. The pattern chart refers to this as 'with nap'.

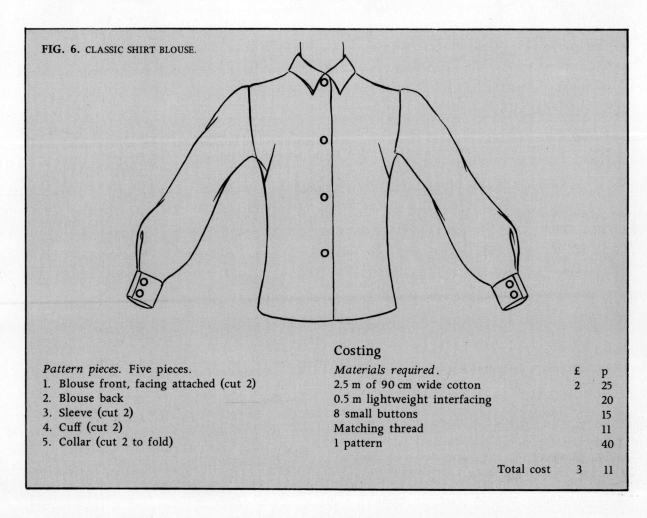

FIG. 6. CLASSIC SHIRT BLOUSE.

Pattern pieces. Five pieces.
1. Blouse front, facing attached (cut 2)
2. Blouse back
3. Sleeve (cut 2)
4. Cuff (cut 2)
5. Collar (cut 2 to fold)

Costing

Materials required.	£	p
2.5 m of 90 cm wide cotton	2	25
0.5 m lightweight interfacing		20
8 small buttons		15
Matching thread		11
1 pattern		40
Total cost	3	11

FIG. 7. LAYOUT ON FABRIC.

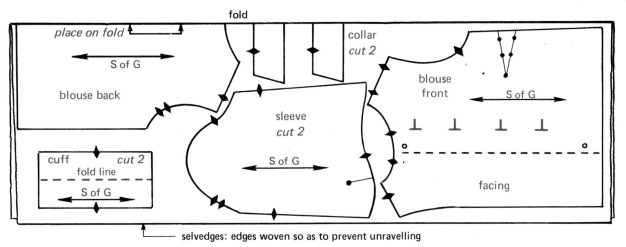

LAYOUT OF PATTERN ON FABRIC

LAYOUT OF PATTERN ON FABRIC

Method

1. Study the instruction sheet giving the layout directions for the style, size, and fabric width.
2. Fold the fabric and lay out the pattern pieces, as directed.
3. Check carefully the following:
   Place fold marks to a fold, S. of G. on grain of fabric. Cut single or double fabric as required.
4. Pin the pattern in the centre of each piece, then smooth it flat and pin carefully along the fitting line, taking special care on corners and curves.
5. Do not cut the fabric before all pattern pieces have been pinned on.

CUTTING OUT

Method

1. Sharp scissors with blades 15 cm long are best. Use the whole length of the blade to give a smooth edge.
2. Keep fabric flat on the table. Cut the notches outwards.
3. Leave all cut-out fabric and pattern pieces pinned together until they are required for use.

MARKING OUT

This can be done by any of three methods:
A. Tailor's chalk.
B. Dressmaker's carbon paper and tracing wheel.
C. Tailor's tacks and thread marking.
Tailor's tacks and thread marking is by far the best method, as it does not rub off or mark the fabric permanently.

A. Tailor's Chalk
Method

1. Push pins through the pattern and fabric on the construction marks.
2. Mark with chalk on all pieces, over the pins.

B. Dressmaker's Carbon Paper
Method

1. Fold carbon paper in half, with R.S. outwards.
2. Place between the two layers of fabric to be marked.
3. Trace over pattern and fabric with a tracing wheel.

C. Tailor's Tacks and Thread Marking

Method

This is done with a long fine needle (straw) and long double thread. (See Figs. 8 and 9)

1. Using a long thread of double cotton, make a stitch within the construction mark through the pattern and all fabric pieces, leaving ends about 4 cm long.
2. Make a back stitch through the first stitch forming the loop, leave another thread 4 cm long and cut thread. (See Fig. 8a)

FIGS. 8(a) & (b). TAILOR'S TACKS.

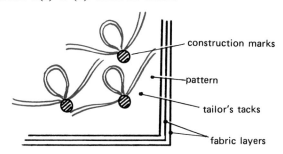

3. Remove pattern gently.
4. Cut tacks between fabrics. (See Fig. 8b)

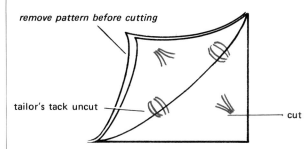

FIG. 9. THREAD MARKING OR TRACE TACKS.

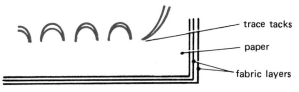

Make these as tailor's tacks, but without loops.
Used for marking straight lines.

Chapter 4

CROSSWAY FABRIC

1. CUTTING
2. JOINING
3. BINDING
4. PIPING
5. FACING

1. CUTTING CROSSWAY STRIPS

Method

1. Fold the fabric in a triangle, so that the **warp** threads lie parallel with the **weft**. (Fig. 10)
2. Press the fold and then cut along it.
3. With chalk and a measure mark the required width of strip from the cut edge, then cut the strips i.e. on true cross grain.

FIG. 10

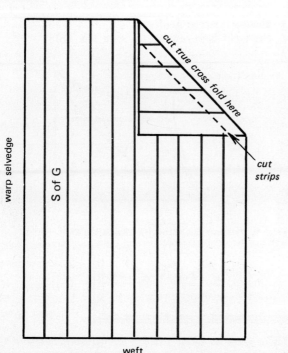

2. JOINING CROSSWAY STRIPS

Method

1. Place strips together R.S. to R.S. on S. of G. edges, so they lie at right angles to each other. (Figs. 11a and b)
2. Pin, tack and stitch 0.5 cm from edges.
3. Remove tacking, press seam open. Trim protruding turnings. (Fig. 11c)

FIG. 11(a)   FIG. 11(b)

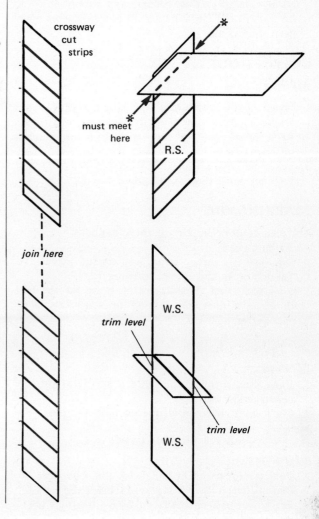

3. CROSSWAY STRIP BINDING

Method

1. Cut a crossway strip four times the finished width of the completed bind.
2. Trim edge to be bound to 0.5 cm from the F.L.
3. Pin, tack and machine the strip 0.5 cm from the edges R.S. to R.S. Stretch strip slightly round corners and outward curves and ease round inward curves. (Fig. 12a)

FIG. 12(a)

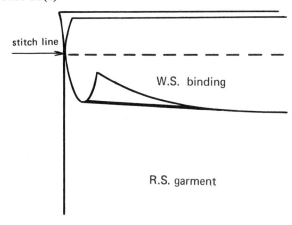

4. Remove tacking. Fold the free edge of the bind snugly over the garment and bind turnings; turn under the edge and pin into position on or just above the stitch line.
5. Hem neatly into position removing pins as you go. (Fig. 12b) Press.

FIG. 12(b)

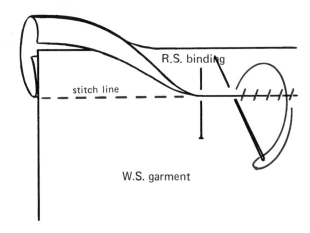

Uses

For all garment edges. This can be both decorative and functional.

4. CROSSWAY STRIP PIPING

Method

1. Cut a crossway strip twice the required width plus turnings.
2. Press strip in half, R.S. outside, stretch slightly and tack together near edges.
3. Place the folded strip between the seam edges and tack on F.L. W.S. through four thicknesses. Stitch and neaten edges if required. (Fig. 13)

FIG. 13

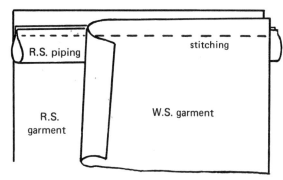

4. Turn seam to R.S. and press piping lightly in required direction.

Uses

For edges to collars, cuffs, waistlines, yokes; also for soft furnishing edges.

5. CROSSWAY FACING

Method

1. Cut a crossway strip the required width plus 1.25 cm for turnings.
2. Pin, tack and machine strip along fitting line on edge to be faced, R.S. to R.S., 0.5 cm from the edge. (Fig. 14a)

FIG. 14(a)

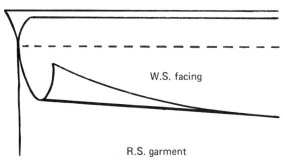

3. Remove tacking and turn facing over to W.S. garment. Work the seam edge out so it lies slightly to the W.S. garment.
4. Turn under 0.5 cm on free edge of strip. Pin and tack flat to the garment W.S. Hem.

FIG. 14(b)

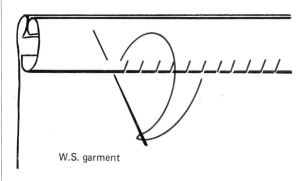

5. Remove tacking and press.

Uses

For facing raw edges when pattern has no shaped facing or hem. As a false hem for lengthening.

Chapter 5

TEXTILE STUDY

Fabrics are divided into two types:

NATURAL

Made from animal and vegetable sources.

MAN-MADE

A. Regenerated cellulose.
B. Synthetically produced from certain materials and chemicals.

NATURAL FIBRES

1. Cotton
2. Linen
3. Wool
4. Silk

MAN-MADE FIBRES

A. Rayon and Acetates

1. Viscose rayon (regenerated cellulose)
2. Acetate
3. Triacetate (Tricel)

B. Synthetics

	Invented by
1. Polyamides	
a) Nylon	American
b) Bri Nylon	British
c) Celon	British
d) Enkalon	Dutch
2. Polyesters	
a) Terylene	British
b) Dacron	American
c) Crimplene	British
3. Acrylics	
a) Acrilan	American
b) Orlon	American
c) Courtelle	British

It is necessary to know the following four facts about all fabrics:
Origin: how it is made and from what.
Properties: how it wears, washes and feels.
Finishes: dyeing, creasing, water and flame proofing, surface finishes.
Uses: articles usually made from it.

NATURAL FIBRES

1. Cotton

Origin
Cotton is grown in every continent, the main producers being U.S.A., China, U.S.S.R., India, Central America and Egypt, though some is grown in Greece, Italy and Spain and a little in Australia. The fluffy white ball of the cotton plant is gathered by hand or machine, and fed into a ginning machine which removes any seeds and also the short fibres called cotton linters (used for making rayon). The longer fibres are baled and shipped to the mills, where they are broken down, beaten, teased and then fluffed by currents of air until they form a large sheet of cotton wool. Another machine removes the impurities and the cotton is then carded and combed into ropes or slivers. The slivers are twisted six at a time then drawn out on a frame to the thickness of one sliver. This process is repeated several times making it thinner still; it is then wound on to bobbins ready for spinning to the thickness required to make yarn and then fabric.

Properties
Strong; hardwearing; can be fine or heavy; strong when wet; launders easily; creases readily; dries well; absorbent; mothproof; flammable (burns to an ash).

Finishes
Mercerized: Sheen
Embossed: Raised pattern
Brushed: Fluffy surface
Trubenized: Stiffened
Tebilized: Crease-resistant
Permanent press
Sanforized: Shrink-resistant
Proban: Flame-resistant

Uses
For adults' and children's dresses, blouses, underwear, raincoats, and overalls; soft furnishing; towels; table-cloths.

2. Linen

Origin

Linen is made from the stems of the flax plant grown mostly in France, Belgium and Ireland. The plants are gathered, left to dry, stripped of leaves and then left for the woody outer parts of the stem to rot away, leaving the long fibres. These are again left to dry. Machines are used to remove impurities and the shorter fibres, and to comb and straighten the long fibres. These are then formed into slivers and treated as cotton.

Properties

Strong; hardwearing; strong when wet; launders easily; creases; frays easily; absorbent; flammable.

Finishes

Sheen, crease-resistant, flameproof, waterproof.

Uses

For adults' and children's dresses, coats, suits, blouses; household linens, i.e. sheets, towels, handkerchiefs, etc.

3. Wool

Origin

Most wool comes from the fleece of sheep from Australia and New Zealand, which are the most productive countries.

The fleece is shorn from the sheep, thoroughly washed, and the long fibres separated from the short ones. The long fibres are combed, divided into slivers, combed again, drawn, twisted then combed again. The slivers are then twisted together six at a time and drawn ready for spinning into yarn, and then woven into fabric. The short fibres require more carding before this process, and produce a rougher material when finished.

Properties

Comfortable, warm, has elasticity and keeps shape, absorbent. Wool must be washed or cleaned with great care. Can be machine washed when treated (Dylan). It burns but does not flare.

Finishes

Mothproof (Dielmoth), showerproof, machine washable, shrink resistant, permanent press.

Uses

For adults' and children's outer and underwear, socks and sweaters; soft furnishing, carpets.

4. Silk

Origin

The silk moth feeds on mulberry leaves; it spins a cocoon which is composed of a continuous filament of fibre called silk. The chrysalis inside the cocoon is killed by heat and the cocoon is then steeped in hot water to allow the filament to unwind. These threads are very fine, so several cocoons are unwound together to form one thread, known as raw silk.

The raw silk is doubled and twisted into a stronger thread; it must be thoroughly washed and boiled in soapy water to remove the gum it contains, and it can then be dyed, dried and woven.

Properties

Non-irritant, has good insulation, has elasticity, strong, absorbent. Must be washed with care.

Finishes

Weighted (addition of metallic salts). Dyed.

Uses

Adult's garments, scarves and ties; curtains and carpets.

MAN-MADE FIBRES

A. Rayon and Acetates

1. Viscose rayon

Origin

Made from wood pulp, carbon disulphide and caustic soda. Processed until it becomes a thick fluid, which is then forced through tiny holes into a bath of sulphuric acid. This hardens the filaments, which are then washed, wound and woven into fabric.

Properties

Soft, weak when wet, washes well, dyes well, absorbent, moth and mildew proof, flammable. A cool iron must be used.

Finishes

Flameproof, crease-resistant, brushed.

Uses

Adults' and children's outer and underwear; curtains, carpets. Blends well with a stronger fibre.

Rayon is inexpensive.

2. Acetate

Origin

Made from cotton fibres too short to be used in the manufacture of ordinary cotton. The cotton is left in acetic acid until it dissolves; it is then dried, added to acetone and mixed to a thick fluid, which is then treated as Viscose Rayon. Wood pulp may replace cotton.

Properties

Soft, weak when wet, washes well, drapes well, creases hang out. A cool iron must be used.

Finishes

Brushed, crease-resistant, flameproof.

Uses

As Viscose rayon

3. Triacetate (Tricel)

Origin

The same as acetate rayon, except that methylene chloride is used instead of acetic acid.

Properties

Will drip dry and needs little ironing as it is less absorbent than other rayons. Crease-resisting, can be permanently pleated. Needs more care in dyeing.

Finishes

Permanent press, crease-resistant.

Uses

As other rayons.

B. Synthetics

1. Polyamides

a) Nylon   b) Bri Nylon   c) Celon   d) Enkalon

Origin

Made from oxygen and nitrogen from air, and hydrogen from water, plus benzine from coal. These ingredients are heated to form a fluid, which is cooled to produce a sheet called polymer. This is broken up into small chips then melted to a thick fluid which is forced through tiny holes forming a filament. The filament is air cooled and wound onto spools, drawn and stretched to four times its length; this gives a fine strong yarn.

Properties

Strong, has elasticity, light weight, resists abrasion, thermoplastic, easy to launder, drip dries, non-absorbent, moth and mildew proof, melts under heat, rots and fades in sunlight. A cool iron must be used.

Finishes

Crimped (gives elasticity), bulked (gives warmth), permanent press.

Uses

Adults' and children's outer and underwear; carpets, curtains, industrial goods, overalls.

2. Polyesters

a) Terylene   b) Dacron   c) Crimplene

Origin

By-products from petroleum, i.e. ethylene glycol and terephthalic acid. These are processed to form a liquid as nylon.

Properties

Holds shape, non-absorbent, moth and mildew proof, melts under heat, crease-resistant, resists sunlight deterioration, electrostatic.

Finishes

Crimped, bulked, permanent press.

Uses

As nylon.

3. Acrylics

a) Acrilan   b) Orlon   c) Courtelle

Origin

Made from coal, natural gas and oil, called acrylonitrile when chemically combined. This is then produced in the same way as nylon, but crimped to give a wool-like texture.

Properties

Non-irritant, warm, strong, lightweight, launders well, crease-resistant, drip dries, melts under heat. A cool iron without steam must be used.

Finishes

Bulked, permanent press.

Uses

Substitute for wool.

FABRIC WEAVES

Plain Weave

The threads are woven evenly over and under warp (the lengthwise threads) and weft (the cross-threads).

Satin Weave

Gives a smooth shiny surface.

Jacquard Weave

Forms a self-design, e.g. brocade, tapestry, damask.

Twill Weave

The fabric has a diagonal cord, e.g. gaberdine, foulard, denim, etc.

Velvet or Pile Weave

A loop-surface weave, which is then cut to give a pile; or fabrics may be woven face to face and then cut.

Slub Weave

Any weave from an uneven fibre, giving a slub or rough surface.

Basket Weave

As plain weave, but two threads over and under the warp and weft.

Knitted Fabrics

A series of loops, worked on a knitting machine.

INTERFACING

This is required to give stiffness and body to collars, cuffs, facings, hems, waistbands and pockets. The interfacing should never be heavier than the fabric with which it is used.

Woven Interfacing

Linen

Lawn

Canvas

Organdie

Net

These interfacings have a warp and weft plain weave, and must be cut on the same grain as the garment, unless direct cross grain is needed for stretching. Woven interfacing requires skill in use, as it can be shaped and moulded under skilful fingers.

Non-woven Interfacing

This is bonded like felt, and has no grain. It comes in all weights, and in white, black and several colours.

Iron-on Interfacing

This can be woven or non-woven with a gum backing that sticks to the fabric when a hot iron is used. Available in all weights.

BASIC FABRICS

Cotton	Characteristics	Uses
Lawn	Fine and soft	Blouses, underwear.
Poplin	Medium weight	Blouses, dresses.
Cambric	Medium to heavy, coarse	Sheets.
Voile	Fine and soft	Blouses, dresses.
Denim	Twill weave	Slacks, skirts, jackets.
Velvet	Pile weave, marks less	Suits, slacks, coats.

Linen	Characteristics	Uses
Lawn	Fine, crisp	Blouses, underwear.
Dress weight	Medium weight	Dresses, suits.
Terylene and linen blend	Crease resistant	Dresses, suits.

Silk	Characteristics	Uses
Jap silk	Fine	Linings.
Foulard	Twill weave	Scarves, dresses.
Wild silk	Slub weave	Coats, suits, evening wear.
Shantung	Rough silk	Blouses, suits, dresses.

Nylon	Characteristics	Uses
Taffeta	Fine and crisp	Linings.
Seersucker	Crinkly, non-iron	Nightdresses, blouses, children's wear.
Jersey	Knitted	Underwear, blouses evening wear.
Brushed	Knitted and textured	Nightwear, evening wear.

Wool	Characteristics	Uses
Flannel	Soft and warm	Suits, coats, slacks.
Tweed	Rough or smooth	Suits, coats, slacks.
Jersey	Stretch knitted fabric	Suits, dresses, slacks.

Terylene	Characteristics	Uses
Suiting	Firm and resilient	Suits, slacks.
Net	Rot proof	Curtains.

Acrilan
Courtelle
Orlon

Rayon	Characteristics	Uses
Brushed	Woven and textured	Dresses.
Velvet	Lustrous, marks easily	Evening wear.
Brocade	Jacquard weave	Evening wear.
Satin	Lustrous, smooth	Evening wear.

FABRIC WIDTHS

36''	90 cm	Most light dress fabrics.
45''	115 cm	Evening materials and some linings.
54''	140 cm	Woollens and jerseys.
60''	150 cm	Jerseys and nets.

Different fibres are woven together to give better wear, appearance, texture, cost, and washability. Constant experiment goes on in this field to improve results.

Chapter 6

PRESSING PROCESSES

Equipment:– See Chapter 1, page 1.

Golden Rules

1. Press each process before starting the next.
2. Remove tacking and pins before pressing.
3. The iron must be lifted and lowered, not pushed along.
4. Test fabric before pressing for reaction to heat and moisture.
5. Good pressing is not over-pressing.

FABRIC PRESSING GUIDE

Cotton:– Hot iron, right or wrong side.
Linen:– Hot iron, W.S. slightly damp.
Wool:– Medium heat, W.S. over damp cloth or using steam iron.
Silk:– Medium heat, W.S. slightly damp.
Nylon:– Little pressing required, cool iron, dry.
Terylene:– Little pressing required, cool iron, dry.
Acrilan:– Little pressing required, cool iron, dry.
Rayon:– Cool iron, W.S. sometimes damp.
Tricel:– Warm iron, W.S. sometimes damp.

PRESSING DARTS

Method

1. Press in following directions:
   Bust darts: down towards waist.
   Neck, shoulder and waist darts: towards the centre of the garment.
   Other darts: as they lie at the wide end.
2. Use a tailor's cushion, sleeve or skirt board point to press darts over.
3. First press along the stitching, each side, to avoid making a fold in the seam. Then press flat in the required direction on the W.S.
4. Care should be taken that the imprint of the fold does not show on the R.S. This can be avoided by placing a piece of soft fabric under the fold of the dart while pressing.
5. Points of darts can be shrunk on the W.S. over a damp cloth on suitable fabrics, e.g. wool, rayon, cotton, etc.

PRESSING SEAMS

Method

1. Place the seam W.S. up, on a skirt board so that no other part of the garment is beneath it.
2. Open up down the seam centre with the iron tip.
3. Now press flat according to the fabric.
4. On heavy fabrics, the heat or steam can be banged out of the seam with a heavy piece of wood: this causes it to 'set'.
5. A roller should be used on fine or soft fabrics to avoid the imprint of the seam edge showing through on the R.S. (Fig. 15).

FIG. 15

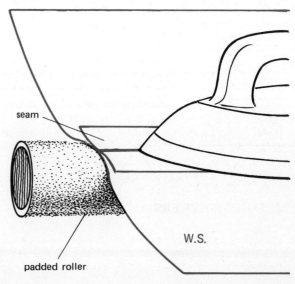

seam

W.S.

padded roller

PRESSING PLEATS

Method

1. When pleats are tacked into position, press each fold separately.
2. Press the whole pleating lightly over a damp cloth.
3. Remove tacking.
4. Press again more firmly, using a damp cloth on the R.S.
5. Hang garment up, and leave to 'set'.

14

FIG. 16

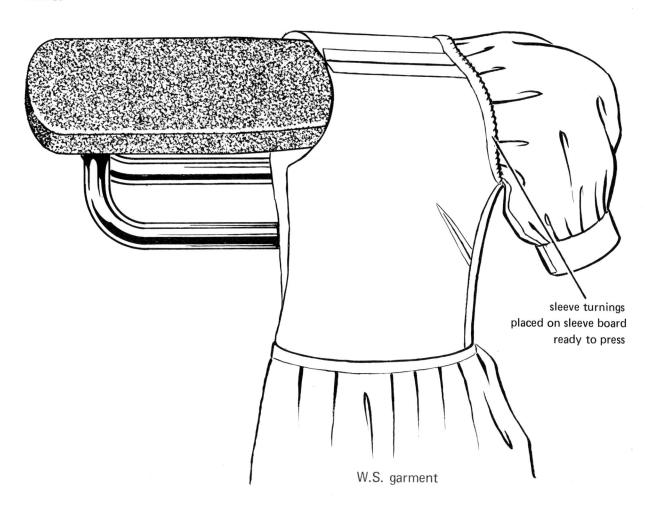

sleeve turnings
placed on sleeve board
ready to press

W.S. garment

PRESSING ARMHOLE SEAMS

Method

1. Use a tailor's cushion or a sleeve board; arrange the armhole seam over this, R.S. downwards, without creasing the sleeve and with the turnings pointing towards the sleeve (Fig. 16).
2. Press a section at a time, working the armhole round as you go.
3. This can also be done on the R.S. over a cloth.
4. Never over-press an armhole seam.

PRESSING GATHERS

Method

1. Press into the gathers with the tip of the iron, pulling the gathered edge away from the iron as you press.
2. Never press gathers flat.

PRESSING TUCKS

Method

1. On the R.S. of the garment, press the underside of each tuck. Do not press past the stitch line.
2. If the tucks are very narrow, stand the iron up on its end and draw the wrong side of the tucks firmly along the surface of the iron.

SHRINKING FULLNESS

(Shaped hems, dart points, etc.)

Method

1. If any imprint is likely to show through on the R.S., place a piece of soft cloth under the fabric.
2. Place a fairly damp cloth over the W.S. of the fabric.
3. Pass the hot iron lightly over the surface, causing the steam to shrink the required part.
4. Press more firmly until dry.

PRESSING VELVET

Cotton velvet can be pressed on the W.S. lightly with a cool iron. Other velvets are best pressed over a velvet board made for this purpose. This board has fine wire spikes all over its surface, and the pile side is laid over these and lightly pressed. Seams and processes can also be pressed by standing the iron up on end and pulling the W.S. of the section firmly across the surface of the iron.

FINAL PRESS ON W.S.

1. Press sleeves, collar, cuffs and trimmings.
2. Press bodice.
3. Press skirt.

Never press any part double; never over-press.

Chapter 7

SEAMS

1. PLAIN SEAM
2. FRENCH SEAM
3. DOUBLE STITCHED SEAM
4. RUN AND FELL SEAM
5. OVERLAID SEAM

1. PLAIN SEAM

Method

Stage I (Fig. 17a)

1. Place two sections R.S. together.
2. Pin, tack, machine on fitting line.
3. Neaten ends, remove tacking.

Stage II (Fig. 17b)

1. Press turnings open with the iron tip, then press flat.
2. Neaten according to fabric.

FIG. 17(a)   **FIG. 17(b)**

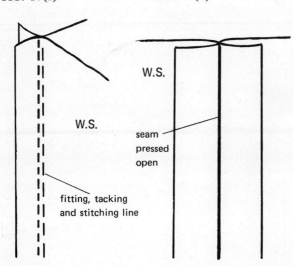

Uses

For most fabrics except transparent ones; wherever inconspicuous flatness is required.

Plain Seam Neatenings

Five Methods

Method A

Edges turned under and stitched.
1. Turn under raw edges 0.5 cm.
2. Machine along this edge.

FIG. 18

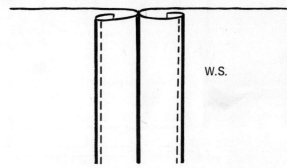

Uses

Cottons, non-transparent silks and lightweight man-made fibres.

Method B

Raw edges oversewn.

FIG. 19

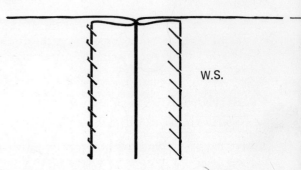

Uses

Firm materials.

Method C

Machined (zig-zag stitched) raw edges.

FIG. 20

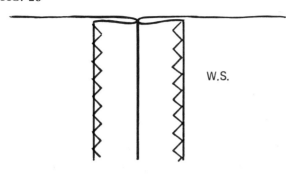

Uses

Stretch fabrics and most others.

Method D

Loopstitched raw edges.

FIG. 21

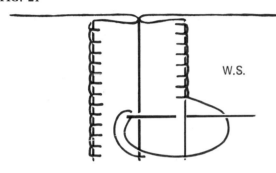

Uses

Stretch fabrics and most others

FIG. 22(a)

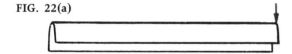

Method E

Binding edges
1. Press binding a fraction less than in half.
2. Place longer section underneath raw edge of seam turning, and fold shorter section over to the R.S. and tack.
3. Stitch into position with machine, being sure to catch in all edges.
4. Remove tacking and press.
Straight or crossway binding may be used.

FIG. 22(b)

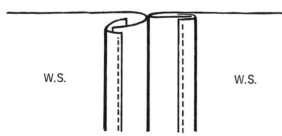

Uses

For heavier fabrics that fray easily.

2. FRENCH SEAM

Method

Stage I

1. Place fabric R.S. together.
2. Pin and tack along fitting line.
3. Stitch 0.5 cm from the F.L.
4. Trim turnings down to less than 0.5 cm.
5. Remove tacking and press seam open.

FIG. 23(a)

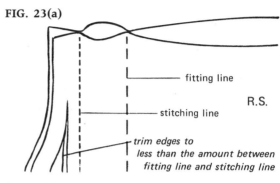

Stage II

1. Turn seam to W.S.
2. Press seam thicknesses together without any groove.
3. Pin, tack and stitch 0.5 cm from first stitching.
4. Remove tacking.
5. Press flat.

FIG. 23(b)

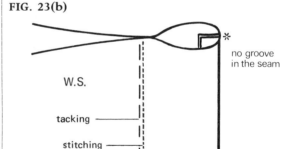

Uses

For fine or transparent fabrics which require frequent laundering (this seam is self-neatening).

3. DOUBLE STITCHED SEAM

Method

Stage I

1. Pin, tack and stitch fabric R.S. together.
2. Remove tacking.

FIG. 24(a)

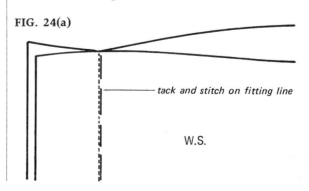

Stage II

1. Trim the turning of back section to half its width.
2. Fold the front turning over to meet the trimmed turning.

FIG. 24(b)

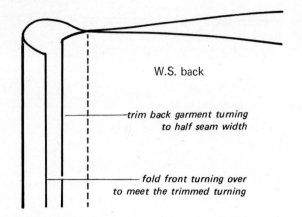

W.S. back

trim back garment turning
to half seam width

fold front turning over
to meet the trimmed turning

Stage III

1. Pin and tack the front turning, with fold, flat to the back section.
2. Top stitch along the fold edge through all thicknesses.
3. Remove tacking and press.

FIG. 24(c)

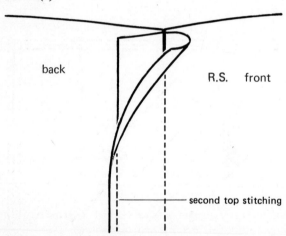

back

R.S.   front

second top stitching

4. RUN AND FELL SEAM

This seam is worked in exactly the same way as the one above but is done by hand, starting on the opposite side, i.e. W.S. together.

Uses

For garments where a flat, self-neatening, hard wearing seam is required, i.e. overalls, jeans, bras, etc.

5. OVERLAID SEAM

Method

Stage I

1. Turn the upper section under on the F.L. to the W.S. and press.
2. Place this section on top of the lower section on R.S., with F.L.s meeting.
3. Pin, tack and top stitch along this edge. Remove tacking and press.

FIG. 25(a)

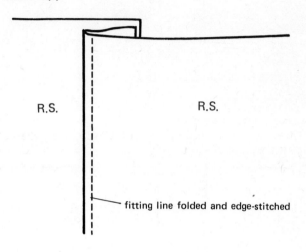

R.S.   R.S.

fitting line folded and edge-stitched

Stage II

1. Neaten two raw edges together with loop stitch on W.S.

FIG. 25(b)

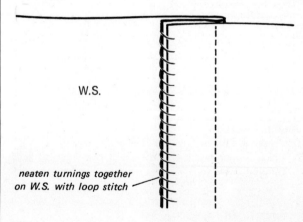

W.S.

neaten turnings together
on W.S. with loop stitch

Uses

This is a conspicuous seam to be used where top stitching is desired, e.g. yokes, waistlines, stylelines. The edge stitching can form a tuck if wished.

Chapter 8

ASSEMBLING AND FITTING

Before assembling garments, tack all pieces together to check fitting. When tacking, always start and end with a double back stitch.

1. LONG AND SHORT TACKING

Uses
For hems and processes.

FIG. 26

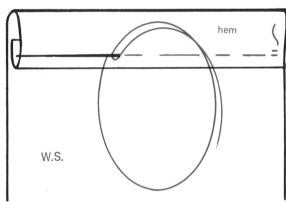

2. EVEN TACKING

Uses
For long seams and hems.

FIG. 27

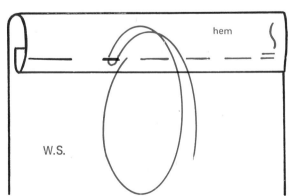

3. BASTING

A horizontal stitch made without turning the work.

Uses
To hold layers of fabric together, i.e. interfacings and linings etc.

FIG. 28

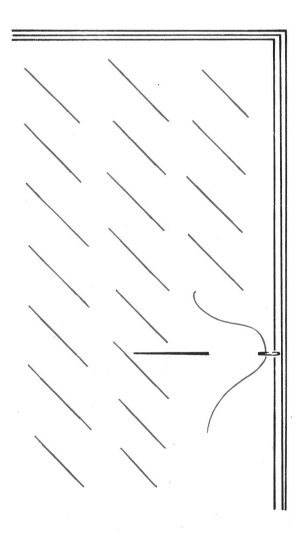

ORDER OF ASSEMBLING GARMENTS

A. Round Method

1. Tack bodice darts
2. Tack shoulder and side seams
3. Fit bodice
4. Stitch and press darts
5. Stitch, neaten and press bodice side seams
6. Apply interfacing to collar, cuffs and fronts
7. Complete collar and cuffs
8. Attach collar
9. Stitch and neaten sleeve seam
10. Attach cuffs
11. Inset sleeves
12. Tack skirt seams together
13. Tack skirt to bodice
14. Second fitting
15. Untack waistline
16. Stitch and neaten skirt seams
17. Retack skirt to bodice, stitch and neaten edges together
18. Hang up garment for some time to allow hem to "drop"
19. Level and complete hem
20. Insert zip fastener
21. Work buttonholes and sew on buttons
22. Final press

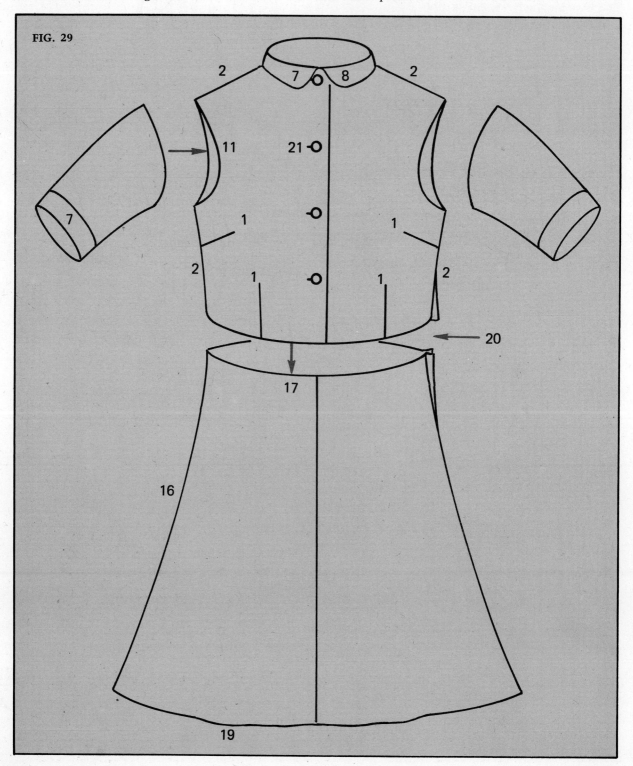

FIG. 29

B. Flat Method

This method resembles mass production and is only used for simple garments that require little fitting.

1 Join style seams and darts, press.
2. Join shoulder seams and neaten, press.
3. Complete neckline.
4. Set in sleeve.
5. Tack and fit C.B. and side seams.
6. Insert zip fastener.
7. Level and complete hem.
8. Final press.

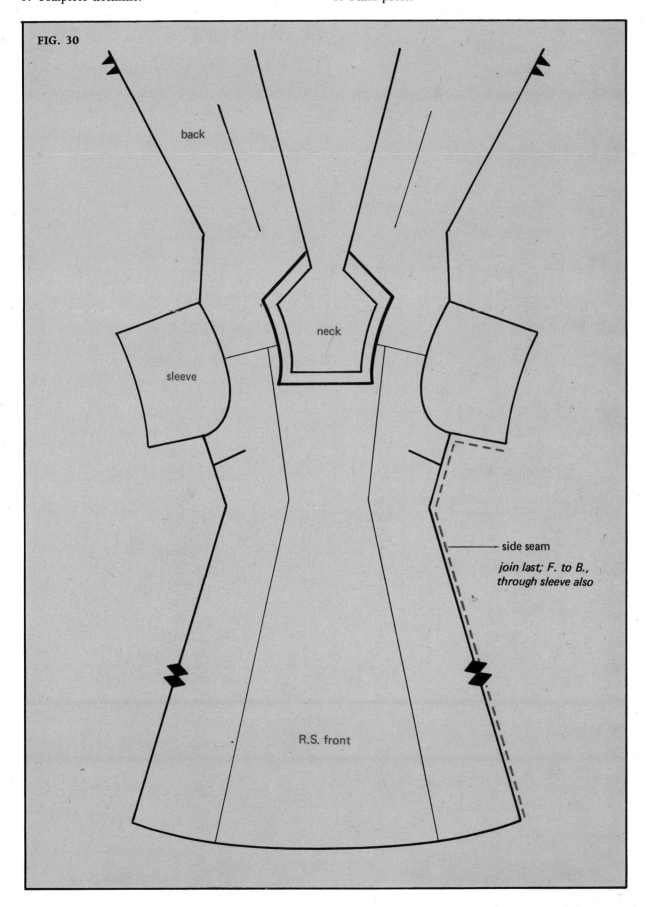

FIG. 30

back

neck

sleeve

side seam
*join last; F. to B.,
through sleeve also*

R.S. front

FITTING CORRECTIONS

Bodice Corrections

Fit over underwear; allow ease for movement; take even amounts each side.

If the wearer has equal measurements on left and right side, fitting on the W.S. saves correcting through to the R.S. Otherwise the same fitting rules apply and must then be corrected through.

Method A
Transferring Fitting Corrections to W.S.

1. Trace tack through double material over fitting pins on R.S.
2. Remove pins, turn garment to W.S. and cut between tacks. Retack new fitting line.

Method B

1. Turn garment to W.S. and mark back and front with tailor's chalk over pins.
2. Retack new fitting line.

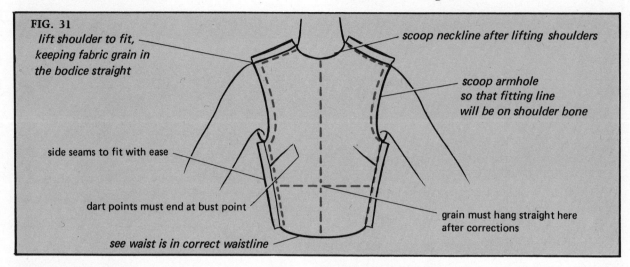

FIG. 31
lift shoulder to fit, keeping fabric grain in the bodice straight

scoop neckline after lifting shoulders

scoop armhole so that fitting line will be on shoulder bone

side seams to fit with ease

dart points must end at bust point

grain must hang straight here after corrections

see waist is in correct waistline

Skirt Corrections

After retacking adjustments fit again on the R.S. Correct the hem only when the rest of the garment is finished.

FIG. 32(a)   **FIG. 32(b)**

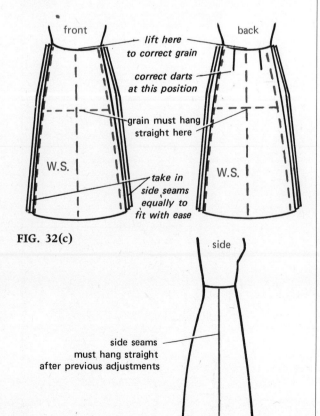

front

back

lift here to correct grain

correct darts at this position

grain must hang straight here

W.S.

W.S.

take in side seams equally to fit with ease

FIG. 32(c)

side

side seams must hang straight after previous adjustments

Sleeve Corrections

Before making sleeve adjustments check that you have the right sleeve in the right armhole.

FIG. 32(d)

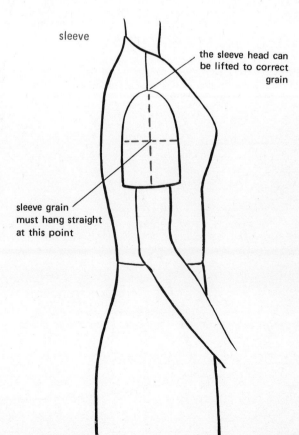

sleeve

the sleeve head can be lifted to correct grain

sleeve grain must hang straight at this point

Chapter 9

OPENINGS

1. CONTINUOUS STRIP OPENING
2. BOUND OPENING
3. FACED OPENING
4. WRAP OPENING
5. ZIP OPENING

1. CONTINUOUS STRIP OPENING

Openings can be made in
A. Cut slit (Fig. 33)
B. French seam (Fig. 34)
C. Open seam (Fig. 35)

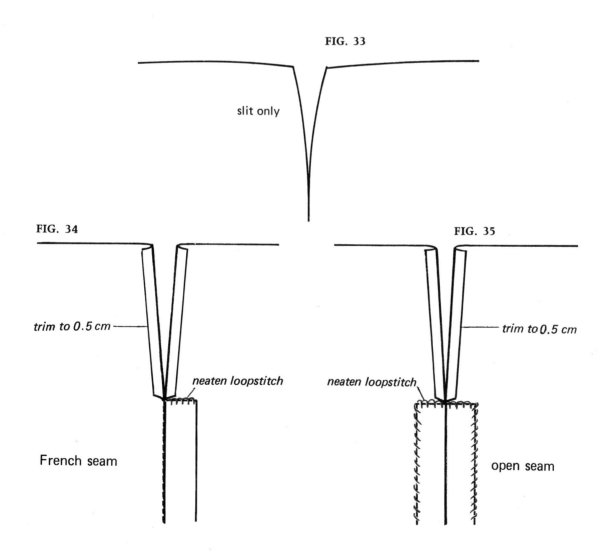

FIG. 33

slit only

FIG. 34

trim to 0.5 cm

neaten loopstitch

French seam

FIG. 35

trim to 0.5 cm

neaten loopstitch

open seam

Method

1. Cut a strip of fabric twice the opening length, twice the finished width, plus 1 cm turnings.
2. Open out slit till horizontal. Tack and stitch strip along the opening R.S. to R.S., starting and ending with 1 cm turnings, narrowing to only 0.25 cm at the centre. This avoids a pucker.

FIG. 36(a)

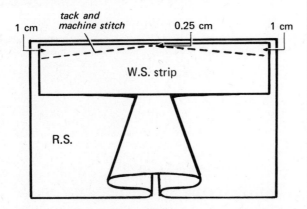

3. Press a turning of 1 cm over to W.S. of the free side of the strip, and bring this edge over to the machine stitching. Pin into position, tack, hem and press.

FIG. 36(b)

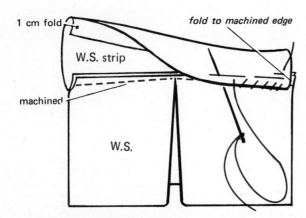

4. Fold back half of the finished strip to the W.S.
5. Bring the top half of the strip to lie over the folded back bottom half.

FIG. 36(c)

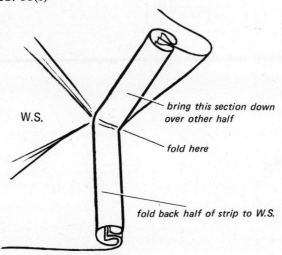

6. Continuous strip opening completed on R.S.

FIG. 36(d)

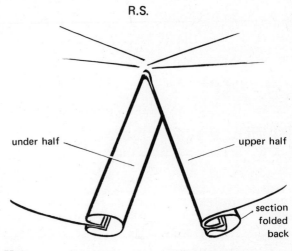

Uses

For sleeves, necks, pyjama trousers, side opening on full skirts.

2. BOUND OPENING

As a continuous strip opening, but instead the strip is cut on cross grain.

Uses

As for continuous strip opening, but more on lightweight and transparent fabrics.

3. FACED OPENING

Method

1. Mark the exact opening with trace tacks.

FIG. 37(a)

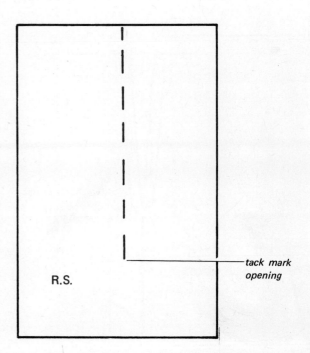

2. Cut a piece of fabric 8 cm wide and 4 cm longer than the opening. Neaten three sides of the facing by turning the edges 0.5 cm to the W.S. and stitch edge by machine.
3. Press a crease down the long centre of the facing, and apply this crease R.S. to R.S. on tack-marked opening. Baste into position.

FIG. 37(b). FACING TACKED AND STITCHED.

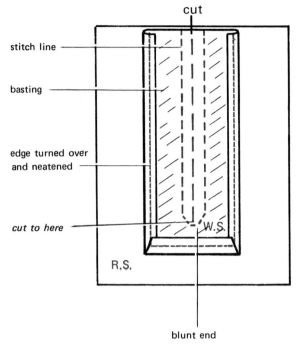

4. Machine down one side of the tack mark on the R.S., make a blunt end, and turn and stitch up the other side of the tack mark (see diagram).
5. Cut through 2 thicknesses to the blunt end but do not cut stitching. Remove tacking, turn facing to R.S. and press.

FIG. 37(c). FACING COMPLETED.

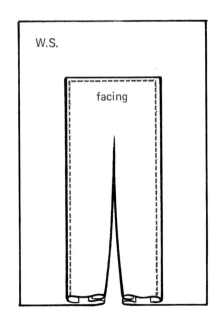

Uses

For sleeve and neck openings with no wrap. Do not use on transparent fabrics.

4. WRAP OPENING

This is a simple opening, where two hems or folds are wrapped one over the other.

FIG. 38(a)

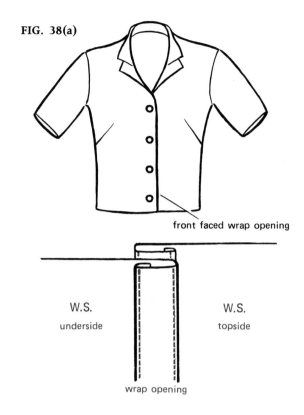

5. ZIP OPENINGS

A. Concealed Zip
B. Even Edge Zip
C. Conspicuous Zip

A. Concealed Zip

FIG. 39(a)

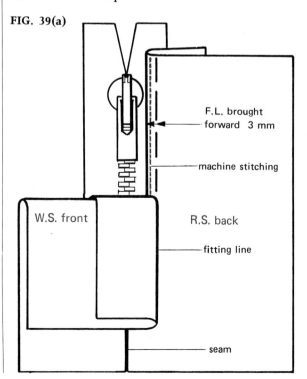

Method

1. Stitch and press open seam below the opening. Press front turning of opening back to F.L. on W.S. Press back turning to W.S. 3 mm outside the F.L.
2. Pin, tack and machine zip to the extended back garment fold.
3. Bring the front F.L. to the back F.L. and tack into position.

FIG. 39(b)

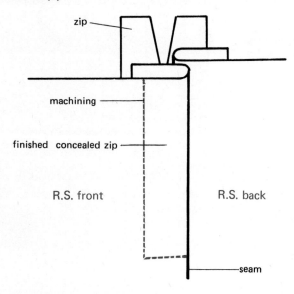

4. Machine stitch over tacking.
5. Remove tacking and press.

Uses

For skirt, C.F. and C.B. dress openings, trouser side and front openings.

B. Even Edge Zip

Set in a skirt side seam.

Method

1. Stitch the left side seam up to the bottom of the opening on the W.S. The opening left should measure the length of the zip plus 1.5 cm.
2. Neaten seam turnings and press open flat on W.S.

FIG. 40(a)

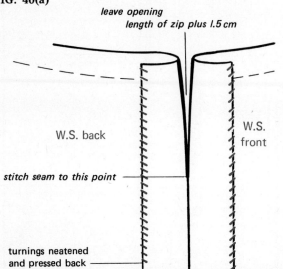

3. Place closed zip tag level with the waist F.L. and so that the opening F.L. is on the zip centre. Pin down one side, and up the other, so that the fitting lines touch.
4. Tack the zip into position 0.5 cm from the F.L.s, then baste the two F.L.s together to avoid slipping.

FIG. 40(b)

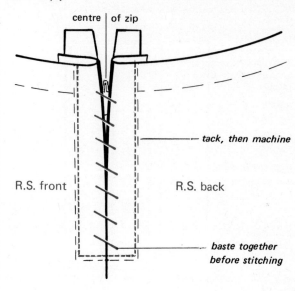

5. Using a zipper foot attachment, machine down and up the tacking on the W.S. lifting the presser foot at the bottom corners. Remove tacking and press.

Uses

All garment openings, cushions, bags, etc.

C. Conspicuous Zip in a Slit

Method

1. Mark the opening length.
2. Mark the fold line both sides 0.5 cm.
3. Cut a square of matching fabric 3 cm square and tack over the end of the opening on R.S. Stitch at marked line.
4. Cut down the opening to 0.5 cm from end, then cut into the corners diagonally, right to the stitching.

FIG. 41(a)

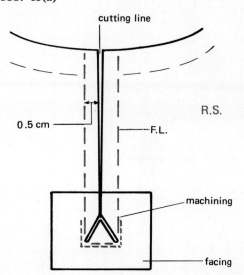

5. Turn the square to the W.S. and press and also press back the turnings to the tack mark on the W.S.

FIG. 41(b)

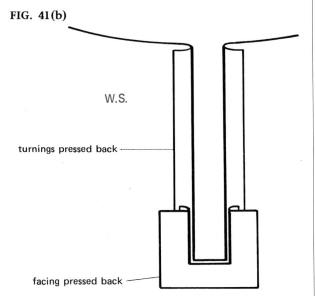

6. Tack the closed zip into the opening R.S., with the tag level with the F.L.

7. Machine zip into position. Remove tacking and press.

FIG. 41(c)

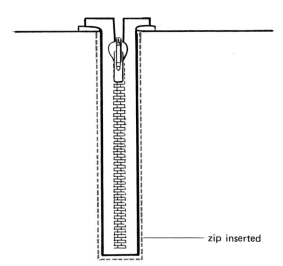

Uses

For openings in sportswear, household articles.

Chapter 10

FASTENINGS

1. **BUTTONHOLES AND BUTTONS**
2. **WORKED LOOPS AND BUTTONS**
3. **EYELET HOLES AND STRINGS**
4. **ROULEAU LOOPS**
5. **HOOKS AND EYES**
6. **PRESS STUDS**
7. **VELCRO**
8. **FROGS**

BUTTONHOLES

Three types: A. Handworked, B. Machined, and C. Bound.

Buttonholes can be horizontal or vertical, worked through at least two thicknesses of fabric.
Buttonholes must measure just a little larger than the diameter of the button, unless the button is thick, when extra length must be allowed. When the position of the buttonhole is marked, it must be at least the width of the button from the edge of the opening. This called the button stand.

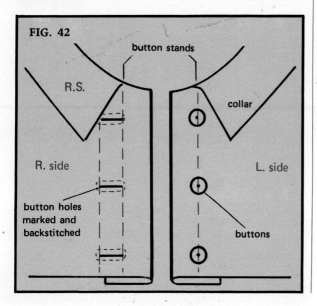

FIG. 42

R.S.

button stands

collar

R. side

L. side

button holes
marked and
backstitched

buttons

A. Handworked Buttonholes

Method

1. The length and position of the buttonholes must be marked in with chalk and tacking evenly spaced, then small back stitching worked round the marks through garment front and facing. An interfacing between these layers is more satisfactory to work with.
2. Cut each buttonhole as you work it with a pair of fine scissors, or buttonhole scissors.
3. Commence working buttonhole stitch from the end farthest from the opening. Bring the needle through the slit to just below the back stitch. Work evenly to the opposite end.

FIG. 43(a)

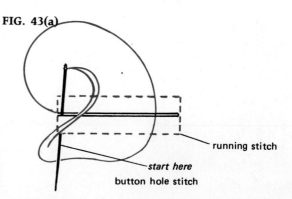

running stitch

start here
button hole stitch

4. The knots of the stitches must lie on the raw edges of the slit.

FIG. 43(b)

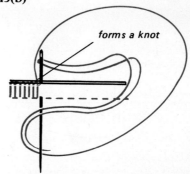

forms a knot

5. Work round the end without knots, fanning the stitches round and continue to buttonhole stitch down the other side.

FIG. 43(c)

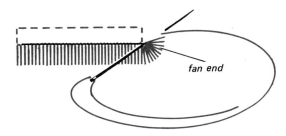

fan end

6. The square end can be worked with a bar, by stitching three times around the end, or buttonhole stitched as diagram shows.

FIG. 43(d)

bar with 3 stitches

FIG. 43(e)

button hole bar

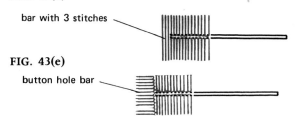

FIG. 43(f)

Uses

Horizontal with one round end: For wrap-front garments.
Vertical: For narrow faced fronts.

B. Machined Buttonholes

These are worked in the same way, but are used on fabrics which fray easily.

C. Bound Buttonholes

Methods

These are done before the neck and hem finishing.
1. Mark the buttonhole size and position, first in chalk, then in running stitch on R.S. through single fabric, so stitches show through on W.S.

FIG. 44(a)

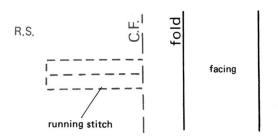

R.S. C.F. fold facing

running stitch

2. Cut a strip of self fabric 5 cm wide, and 2.5 cm longer than the buttonhole. This strip can be S. of G. or true cross. Fold this strip in half lengthwise and place evenly over the marked buttonhole, R.S. to R.S. Open flat and tack into position.

FIG. 44(b)

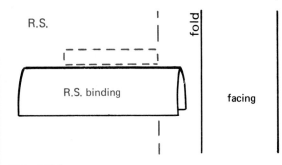

R.S. fold R.S. binding facing

FIG. 44(c)

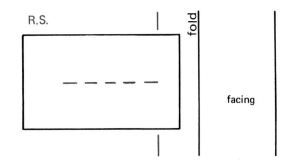

R.S. fold facing

3. Turn work to the W.S. and stitch an exact oblong over the tack marks, counting the end stitches to be sure that they are equal. Always start stitching in the centre.

FIG. 44(d)

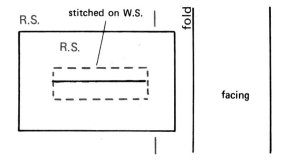

R.S. stitched on W.S. fold R.S. facing

4. Remove tacking and cut through the centre of buttonhole, both thicknesses, to within 0.25 cm of ends, then diagonally into corners, not cutting stitching.

FIG. 44(e)

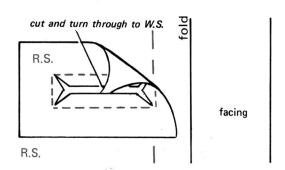

cut and turn through to W.S. fold R.S. facing R.S.

5. Turn facing through to W.S. then wrap closely over the raw edges.
6. Tack bind into position with inverted pleat each end on W.S., oversew pleats to the bind.

FIG. 44(f)

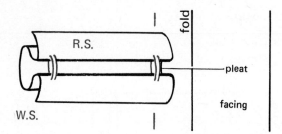

7. Tack bind together on R.S. and stab-stitch along the groove. Fold facing to W.S. Push a pin through each end to W.S. in order to mark position of buttonhole.

FIG. 44(g)

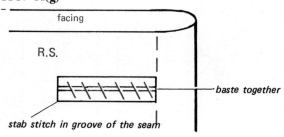

FIG. 44(h)

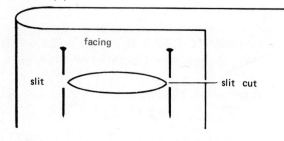

8. Cut a slit through the facing only on the W.S.
9. Turn cut edge under the hem to the bind.

FIG. 44(i)

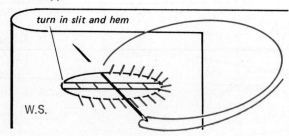

10. Remove tacking and press.

FIG. 44(j)

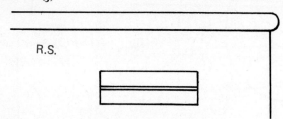

Uses finished bound buttonhole

For non-transparent fabrics, and fabrics that fray badly.

BUTTONS AND SEWING ON BUTTONS
Button shapes are varied.

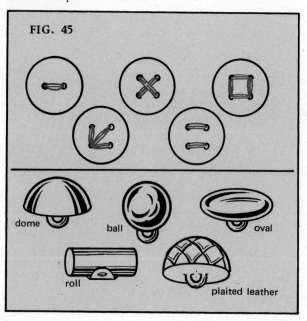

FIG. 45

dome ball oval roll plaited leather

Buttons are made of both synthetic and natural materials, e.g.

Glass	Shell
Metal	Bone
Wood	Cloth
Leather	Plastic

A well-made garment should be complemented with good tasteful buttons.

All buttons should be attached with a shank through double fabric, unless they have a self shank. This avoids puckering when the garment is fastened.

Method

1. Mark button position through the buttonhole round end, where the button will lie when fastened. Fix crossed pins in this spot.

FIG. 46(a)

2. With strong sewing thread according to fabric, sew through the holes, stabbing up and down through button and fabric several times, over the pins.

FIG. 46(b)

3. Remove pins, bring needle up between the button and garment, wind the thread round the shank six times, pass the needle to the back of the facing, and secure with a back stitch.

FIG. 46(c)

shank

2. WORKED LOOPS

Method

1. Mark the loop's position with pins and a measure. The size of the mark should be a little less than the diameter of the bottom. (A loop allows more space than a buttonhole.) Work on faced or double thickness of garment.
2. With double thread back stitch at one mark, and again at the opposite mark, forming a loop. (Test with button for size.) Make another loop the same size in the same place.

FIG. 47(a)

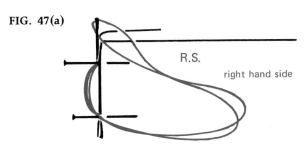

3. Loop stitch closely over the four threads until they are covered. Back stitch end on W.S. and cut thread.

FIG. 47(b)

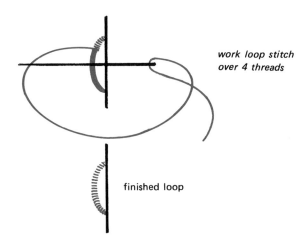

work loop stitch
over 4 threads

finished loop

Uses

For children's clothes, faced openings at necks, underwear.

3. EYELET HOLES

Method

1. Mark the position of the holes with a dot of chalk or pencil on R.S.
2. Work a row of close back stitching around the dot, to size required.

FIG. 48(a)

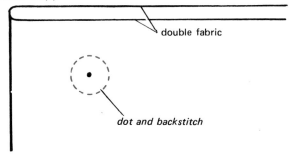

double fabric

dot and backstitch

3. Pierce through the dot with a stiletto to make a clear hole.
4. Oversew closely and evenly around the hole on R.S. over back stitch, drawing back the fabric to the back stitch firmly.

FIG. 48(b)

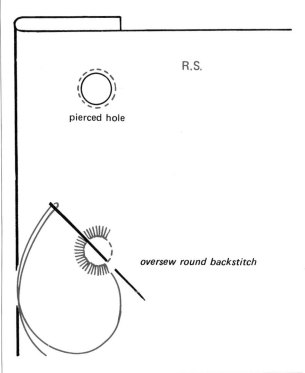

R.S.

pierced hole

oversew round backstitch

FIG. 48(c) EYELET HOLES AND TIE STRING ON A NECKLINE

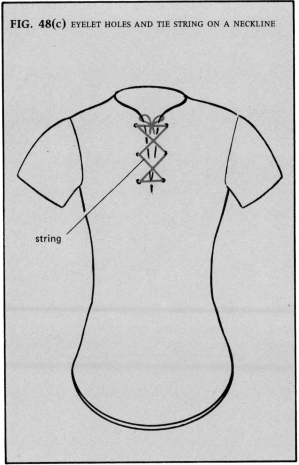

string

Uses

Mainly a fashion feature on fronts and necklines.

4. ROULEAU LOOPS

A. Rouleau Cord for Loops

Method

1. Cut several lengths of true cross fabric strips according to loops required, 2.5 cm wide.
2. Fold the strips in half R.S. inside and machine 0.25 cm from the raw edge.

FIG. 49(a)

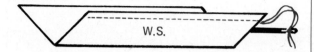

3. Turn tube inside out, by tying a bodkin to the double thread ends, and work the bodkin through the tube.

FIG. 49(b)

B. Attaching the Loops

Method

1. Form and pin the loops along the R.S. opening edge, (as diagram) arranged equally according to the button diameter, with the rouleau seam uppermost. Tack into position on the fitting line.

FIG. 50(a)

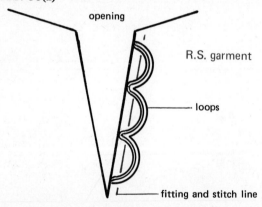

2. Neaten the facing edge. Pin and tack facing into position R.S. to R.S. over the loops.
Tack and stitch on the fitting line.

FIG. 50(b)

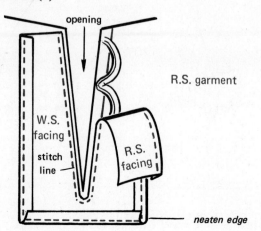

3. Remove tacking, turn the facing to the W.S. The loops will then lie in position.
Press so that the seam edge does not show on the R.S.

FIG. 50(c)

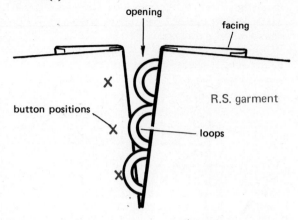

Uses

As a decorative, functional finish on openings. Ball buttons are frequently used with rouleau loops, and care should be taken to try these through the loops for size before stitching.

5. HOOKS AND EYES

Method

1. Place the hook 3 mm back from the overlap edge W.S. Stitch into position round the loops with buttonhole stitch, and overstitch hook end to fabric.
2. The eye should be fixed in the same way, but 3 mm over the edge. Worked and metal bars are marked in according to the wrap required.

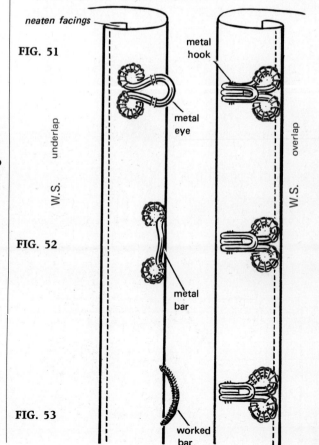

FIG. 51

FIG. 52

FIG. 53

6. PRESS STUDS

Method

1. Pierce pins through closed wrap, R.S. to the underlap in the required position. Now re-mark with chalk dots on R.S. underlap and W.S. overlap. The studs should never lie too near the edge. Oversew through holes to fabric.

FIG. 54

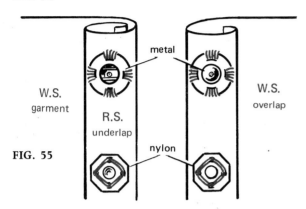

FIG. 55

Uses

Mainly for waistbands or to hold corners down.

7. VELCRO STRIP

Velcro can be stitched each side of the tapes on over- and under-wraps, and holds the opening together by being pressed together. It fastens because the under wrap has a mesh of tiny nylon loops, and the overwrap has a dense nylon pile, and when pressed together it "locks".

When Velcro is used it should be stitched in place before the facings are completed.

FIG. 56

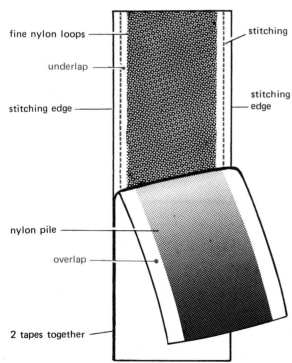

Uses

Mainly for sportswear.

8. FROGS

FIG. 57(a)

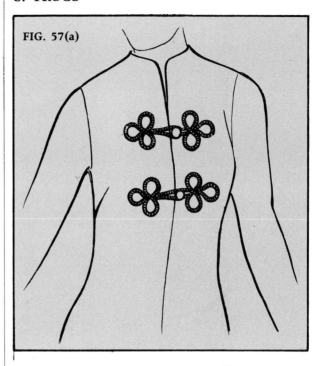

Method

Frogs can be made from twisted rouleau or braid.

1. Chalk in the shape of the frog so that three loops can be twisted to form the shape.
2. Stab stitch the braid or rouleau into position, on R.S. R. Front so the loop extends over the front edge. On the R.S. L. Front the loop must lie as far in from the front edge as wrap over required.

FIG. 57(b)

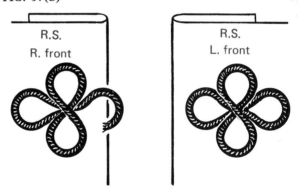

3. Fix a button to the end of the L. Front frog loop and the loop opposite will button over.

FIG. 57(c)

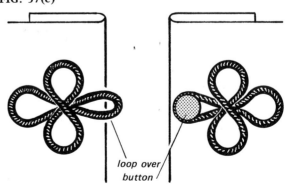

Uses

For decorative fastenings for necks and fronts.

Chapter 11

COLLARS

1. **SHIRT COLLARS (3 METHODS)**
2. **FLAT COLLARS (PETER PAN)**
3. **ROLL COLLARS**
4. **MANDARINE COLLARS**
5. **TURTLE COLLARS**

The above list of collars is basic; any other styles are applied using the same methods.

The collar is applied after the shoulder seams have been completed and neatened, the front or back facings attached and neatened, and the bodice fitted, especially at the neckline. The collar is then made up, usually with interfacing.

MAKING THE COLLAR
Method

1. Baste interfacing to W.S. of one collar section.
2. Place two collar sections together, R.S. to R.S., matching construction marks.
3. Tack together on fitting line, round three sides, leaving the neck edge free.
4. Stitch along tacked edge. (Fig. 58a)
5. Remove tacking and trim turnings down in layers, i.e. Interfacing close to stitching
   Next layer 0.25 cm from stitching
   Last layer 0.5 cm from stitching. (Fig. 58b)
6. Turn collar to R.S.
   Baste through the centre and press. (Fig. 58c)

All shirt collars which need to be attached are made by this method.

FIG. 58(a)

neck edges

interfacing

two collar pieces   R.S. to R.S.

stitch line

FIG. 58(b)

layer each edge

cut off corner

FIG. 58(c)

collar turned to R.S.

R.S.

basting

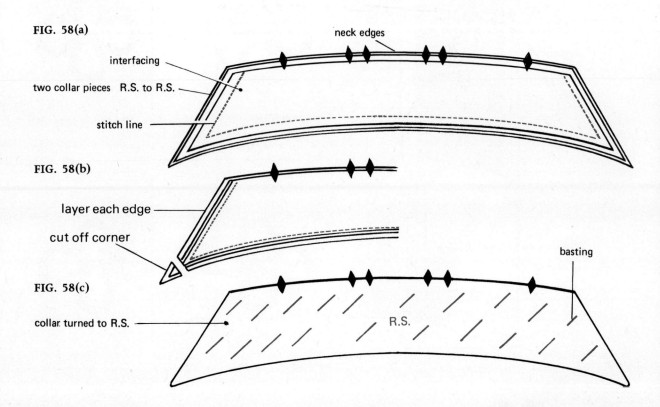

1. SHIRT COLLAR

A. With Front and Back Facing

Method

1. Pin and tack collar across neck of blouse, R.S. to R.S. matching balance marks.
2. Bring completed back neck and front facing over to lie in line with the collar neck edge, R.S. facing to R.S. collar, matching balance marks.
3. Pin, tack and stitch right across through facings, collar and blouse.

FIG. 59(a)

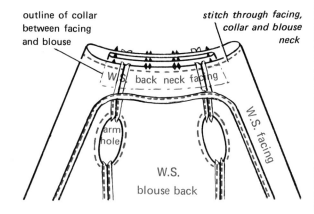

4. Trim turnings down to 0.5 cm.
5. Turn facings over to W.S. blouse. Press and stitch facing seams to shoulder seams.

FIG. 59(b)

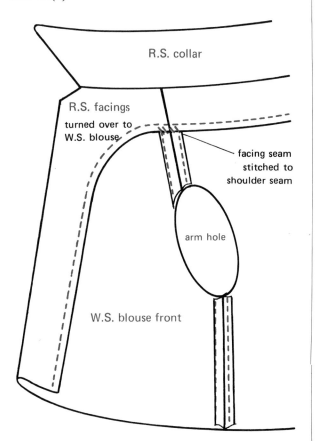

Uses

Collars that need to stand close round the neck and can be open or closed at the neck.

B. Front Facing Only

Method

1. Tack collar to blouse neckline R.S. to R.S. matching balance marks.

FIG. 60(a)

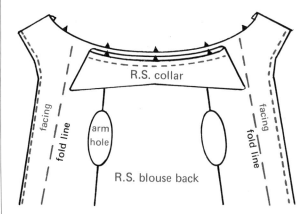

2. Fold neatened front facing back, over collar, matching balance marks.
3. Tack and stitch from fold line to edge of facing, each side.
4. Tack back neck blouse and one section of collar from A to B. Stitch here. (Fig. 60b)

FIG. 60(b)

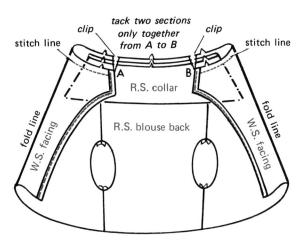

5. Neaten thread ends and trim turnings of neck edge to 0.5 cm. Clip at A and B.
6. Turn facings over to W.S. and press flat with collar.
7. Turn under the raw edge of the collar back neck, and hem to stitching.
8. Hem facing to shoulder seam.

FIG. 60(c)

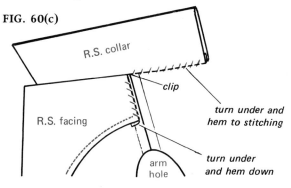

C. Machined R.S. Handstitched W.S.

FIG. 61(a)

COLLAR MADE UP

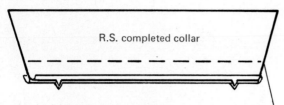

neck edge turnings left unstitched to fitting line

1. Prepare front by stitching across button stand.
2. Clip and trim as diagram.

FIG. 61(b)

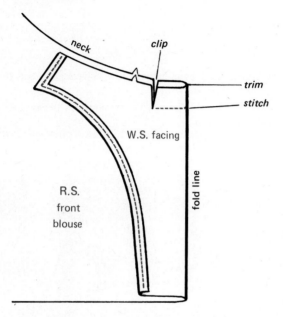

3. Turn facing over to W.S. leaving the neck edge free.

FIG. 61(c)

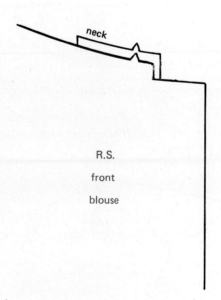

4. Pin, tack and stitch to top section of the collar to W.S. neck edge, over facings, matching balance marks. (Fig. 61d)

FIG. 61(d)

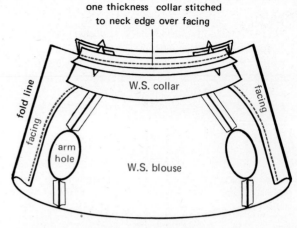

one thickness collar stitched to neck edge over facing

5. Remove tacking, trim turnings to 0.5 cm. Turn under free edge on under collar to meet stitching. Hem down. Press.

FIG. 61(e)

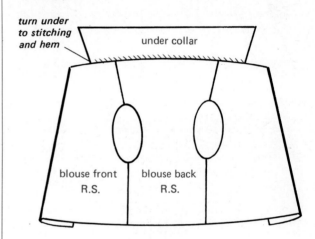

2. FLAT COLLAR (PETER PAN)
Method—Making up Collar

1. Baste interfacing to under collar section.
2. Pin, tack and stitch 2 collar sections together, matching balance marks.
3. Remove tacking, trim, clip, and layer turnings.

FIG. 62(a)

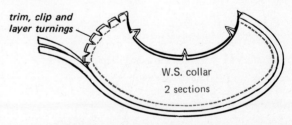

4. Turn collar through to R.S. Tack round outside edge 0.5 cm in so the seam does not show on the R.S. Press lightly.

FIG. 62(b)

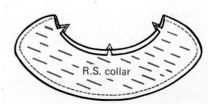

Method—Setting on Collar

1. Pin and tack the completed collar round the neckline R.S. to R.S. over the facings which have been folded to the blouse W.S.

FIG. 63(a)

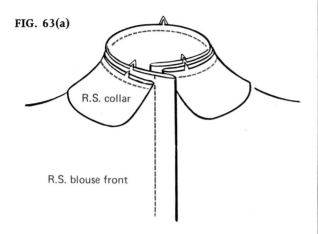

2. Cut a crossway strip of self fabric 2.5 cm wide plus turnings each end.
3. Pin the crossway strip over the collar all round the neck edge R.S. to R.S. on the fitting line. Tack and stitch.

FIG. 63(b)

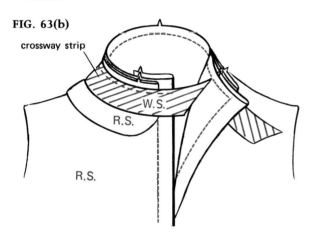

4. Remove tacking, trim turnings to 0.5 cm. Pull collar up and press crossway strip flat over turnings. Turn under free edge of strip and hem flat to blouse all round the neckline. Turn ends under and stitch invisibly.

FIG. 63(c). FINISHED COLLAR PRESSED

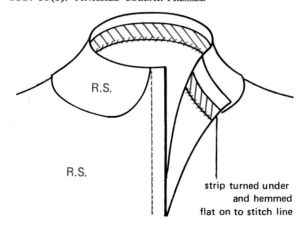

Uses
For most flat collars.

3. ROLL COLLAR
Method

1. Join back of neck of collar and press seam open. Clip at inner shoulders.

FIG. 64(b)

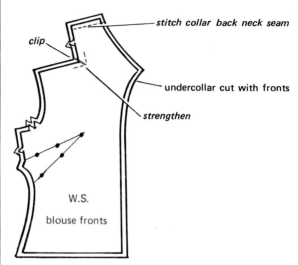

2. Pin, tack and stitch shoulder seams and back neck under-collar.

FIG. 64(b)

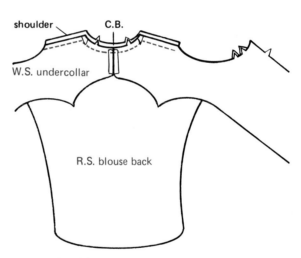

3. Press shoulder seams open.
4. Stitch back neck top-collar and press open.
5. Place top-collar R.S. to R.S. on under-collar, tack, stitch and layer turnings to 0.25 cm and 0.5 cm.

FIG. 64(c)   **FIG. 64(d)**

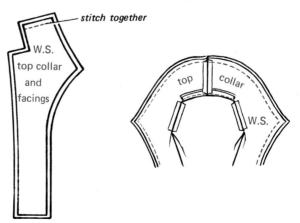

6. Turn collar to R.S. Baste down and hem stitch neck to turnings across back neck.
Completed collar can stand up or down.
The outer edge can be shaped as fashion dictates.

FIG. 64(e)

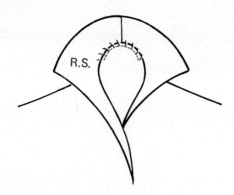

4. MANDARINE COLLAR

This collar is curved.

Method

Apply with all-round facing as shirt collar.

FIG. 65(a)

FIG. 65(b)

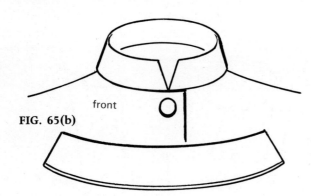

5. TURTLE NECK COLLAR

This collar is straight in shape. It can be cut on straight or cross grain, and is fastened at the back.

Method

Apply with crossway strip or facings.

FIG. 66(a)

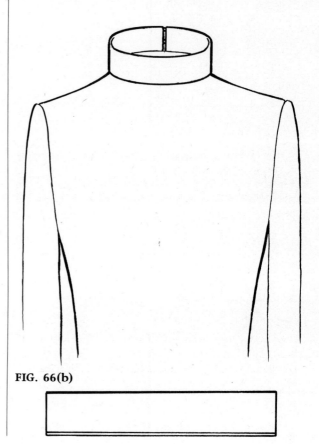

FIG. 66(b)

WILSON MARRIAGE COMPREHENSIVE SCHOOL
COLCHESTER

Chapter 12

CUFFS

1. **SHIRT CUFF**
2. **TURN BACK CUFF**
3. **LINK CUFF**
4. **CIRCULAR CUFF**

1. SHIRT CUFF (with continuous strip opening)

Method

1. *Either* work two rows of gathers on and below the F.L. R.S.
   or pleat as in Fig. 68, matching construction marks.

FIG. 67

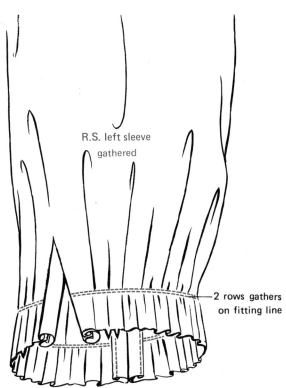

R.S. left sleeve
gathered

—2 rows gathers on fitting line

FIG. 68

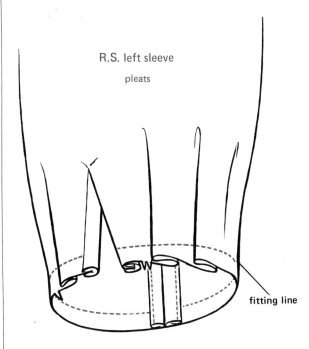

R.S. left sleeve

pleats

fitting line

2. Pull gathers up to fit the cuff.
3. Stitch each end of folded cuff on W.S. as in diagram.
4. Clip and trim turnings.

FIG. 69(a). CUFF.

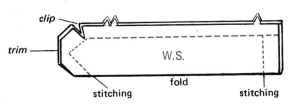

clip

trim

W.S.

fold

stitching

stitching

5. Turn cuff to R.S. and press.

FIG. 69(b). CUFF COMPLETED.

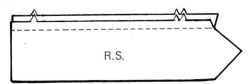

R.S.

6. Pin, then tack one section of the cuff R.S. to R.S. of sleeve end. Adjust gathers as you go. Stitch, remove tacking, trim turnings to 0.5 cm.

FIG. 69(c)

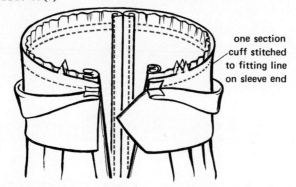

one section cuff stitched to fitting line on sleeve end

7. Pull cuff away from the sleeve and press the turnings into the cuff. Turn under the free cuff edge 0.5 cm to meet the stitch line on W.S. Pin, then hem into position. Press and work buttonhole.

FIG. 69(d)

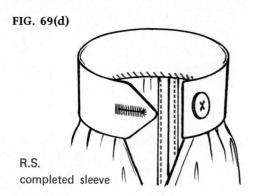

R.S.
completed sleeve

2. TURN BACK CUFF
Method

1. Make cuff by stitching ends on W.S. Trim, turn to R.S. and press.

FIG. 70(a)

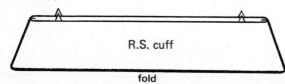

R.S. cuff

fold

2. Pin free edges of cuff round sleeve end R.S. to R.S., matching balance marks.
3. Cut and join a crossway strip 2.5 cm wide. Pin and tack over cuff edges. Stitch, remove tacking and trim to 0.5 cm.

FIG. 70(b)

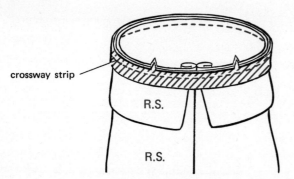

crossway strip

R.S.

R.S.

4. Pull cuff up, turn free edge of crossway strip under and hem flat to the sleeve.

FIG. 70(c)

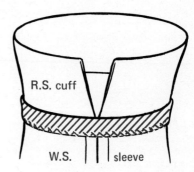

R.S. cuff

W.S. | | sleeve

FIG. 70(d)

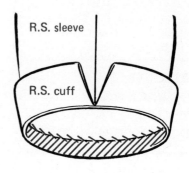

R.S. sleeve

R.S. cuff

3. LINK CUFF
Method

1. Complete faced opening and sleeve seam.
2. Run gather threads along and just below F.L.

FIG. 71(a)

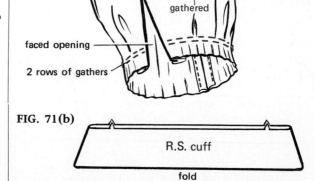

R.S. left sleeve
gathered

faced opening

2 rows of gathers

FIG. 71(b)

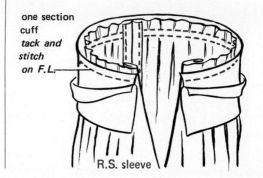

R.S. cuff

fold

3. Make up cuff as for turn back cuff.
4. Pin, tack and stitch top section only of cuff, round F.L. over sleeve gathers, R.S. to R.S.

FIG. 71(c)

one section cuff *tack and stitch on F.L.*

R.S. sleeve

5. Trim turnings to 0.5 cm. Remove tacking.
6. Pull up cuff, away from the sleeve, and press the turnings into the cuff.
7. Turn under and pin the free cuff edge 0.5 cm to meet the stitching on W.S. sleeve. Hem into position and press.
8. Work two buttonholes in cuff to take a link.

FIG. 71(d)

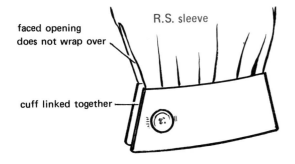

faced opening does not wrap over

R.S. sleeve

cuff linked together

9. Make a link with two buttons.

FIG. 71(e)

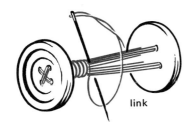

link

4. CIRCULAR CUFF
Method

1. Cut band for cuff on S. of G., twice the desired finished width, and long enough to circle sleeve end, plus turnings.

FIG. 72(a)

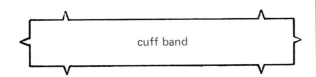

cuff band

2. Join two ends of the band together, R.S. to R.S. on F.L.

FIG. 72(b)

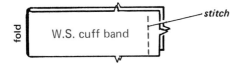

fold

W.S. cuff band

stitch

3. Press turnings open, and fold circle in half to form the cuff.

FIG. 72(c)

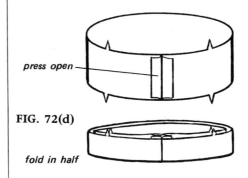

press open

FIG. 72(d)

fold in half

4. Pin, tack and stitch one edge of cuff to the sleeve end, R.S. to R.S. Trim turnings to 0.5 cm. Remove tacking.

FIG. 72(e)

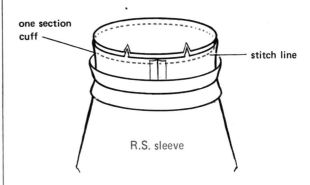

one section cuff

stitch line

R.S. sleeve

5. Pull cuff away from the sleeve, turn under free cuff edge 0.5 cm to W.S. sleeve, pin and hem to stitching line.
6. Press and turn cuff up over sleeve R.S.

Note: This method can also be worked in reverse, i.e. with the hemstitching on R.S. sleeve.

FIG. 72(f)

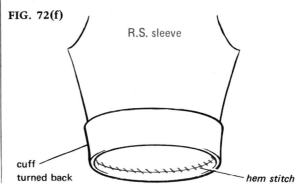

R.S. sleeve

cuff turned back

hem stitch

Chapter 13

FACINGS

1. **SHAPED FACINGS**
2. **STRAIGHT FACINGS**
3. **CROSSWAY FACINGS**
On W.S. facings are functional
on R.S. decorative

1. SHAPED FACINGS
Method

1. Join front and back neck facings together at shoulders, press seams open. Neaten outer edges by turning under 0.5 cm to W.S. and stitching.
2. Pin, tack and stitch neck edge of facing to the garment, R.S. to R.S., matching balance marks.
3. Trim neck edges to 0.5 cm and clip at intervals.

FIG. 73(a)

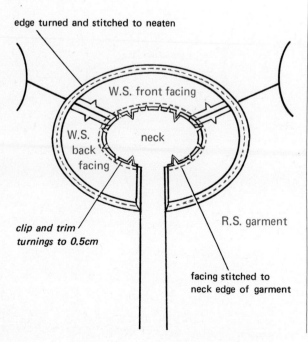

edge turned and stitched to neaten

W.S. front facing

W.S. back facing

neck

R.S. garment

clip and trim
turnings to 0.5cm

facing stitched to
neck edge of garment

4. Turn the facing over to the garment W.S. Press flat so that neck seam does not show on the R.S.

FIG. 73(b)

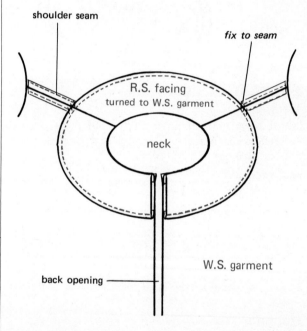

shoulder seam

fix to seam

R.S. facing
turned to W.S. garment

neck

back opening

W.S. garment

5. Hem facing shoulder to garment shoulder, making sure that it does not pull.
6. The armhole can be faced in the same manner. See Fig. 74.

FIG. 74

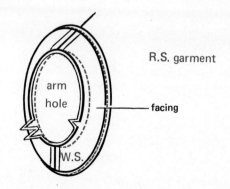

arm hole

R.S. garment

facing

W.S.

2. STRAIGHT FACING
(For straight edges only)

Method

1. Cut a band of fabric, the desired length and width, plus turnings.
2. Fit the band R.S. to R.S. garment, or straight edge to be faced.

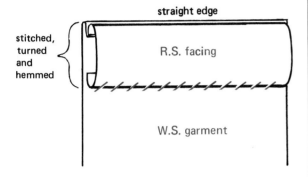

3. If a corner is to be turned, dart the facing to fit, pin, tack and stitch, then cut through the dart or tube, and press open as a seam.
4. The facing is then applied as for a shaped facing.

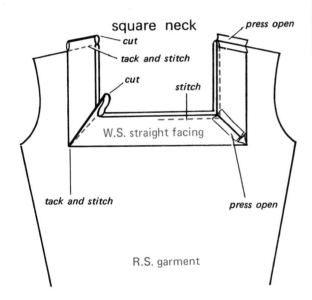

3. CROSSWAY FACING
(For edges with a slight shape or give)

Method

1. Cut a true crossway strip of the required length plus turnings. Make any join which is necessary.
2. Apply facing, as for straight facing, except for a slight stretch on the outward curve, and a slight ease on an inward curve.

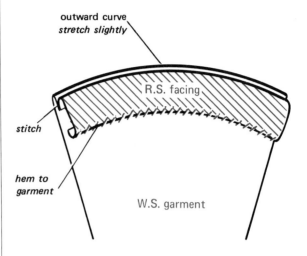

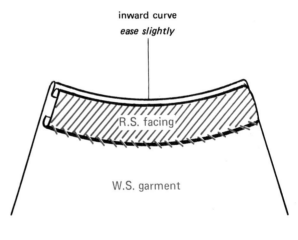

Note: This facing will set better if it is kept narrow.

Chapter 14

SLEEVES

---

1. PREPARATION
2. SETTING IN

---

1. PREPARATION
Method

1. The bodice should be completed and seams neatened and pressed.
2. Check armhole F.L. is correct.
3. Make up a left and right sleeve (check balance marks), neaten and press.
4. Work two rows of fine running stitch round the sleeve head, on and inside the F.L. Attach one end of threads, leaving other ends free to draw in easing.

FIG. 78(a)

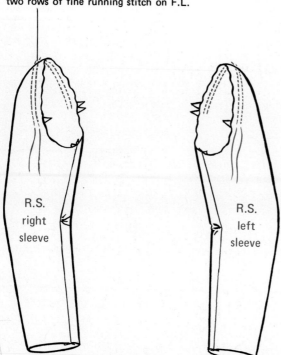

two rows of fine running stitch on F.L.

R.S.
right
sleeve

R.S.
left
sleeve

2. SETTING IN
Method

1. With bodice on its W.S. and sleeve on its R.S., put the sleeve into its correct armhole, R.S. to R.S. bodice, matching balance marks.
2. Working on the sleeve side, pin it into the bodice armhole, easing the fullness slightly at the head. Tack firmly round the armhole F.L.
3. Refit sleeves to check they hang correctly, then stitch round F.L.

FIG. 78(b)

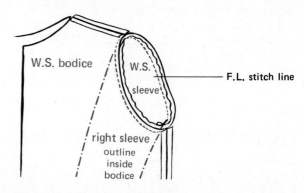

W.S. bodice

W.S.
sleeve

F.L. stitch line

right sleeve
outline
inside
bodice

4. Remove tacking, trim turnings to 1 cm. Neaten edges together with loop stitch or machine zig-zag if to be unlined.
5. Press seam into the armhole.

FIG. 78(c)

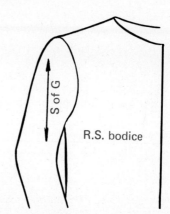

S of G

R.S. bodice

1. RAGLAN
2. DOLMAN
3. FLARED CAPE
4. BISHOP
5. PUFF
6. CAP

1. RAGLAN SLEEVE
Method

1. Pin, tack and stitch sleeve back to bodice back, R.S. to R.S., also sleeve front, R.S. to R.S., on F.L.

FIG. 79(a)

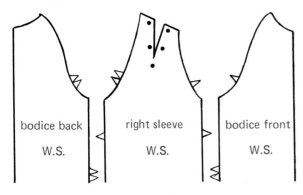

2. Remove tacking, neaten according to fabric unless to be lined.
3. Press seams open.

FIG. 79(b)

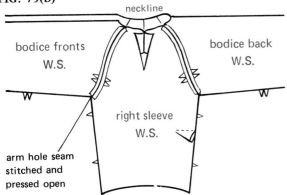

4. Pin back and front of sleeve seams together, also bodice sides on F.L. Tack.
5. Stitch on F.L. continuously through bodice and sleeves.

FIG. 79(c)

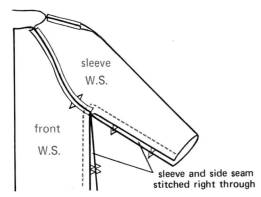

6. Remove tacking and press open, neaten if required.

2. DOLMAN SLEEVE
Method

1. Complete bodice dart.
2. Cut four crossway strips, 3 cm wide and 10 cm long.
3. Neaten strip edges with machine zig-zag or use tape.
4. Tack each strip along each underarm edge on W.S.
5. Pin front and back sleeve seams and bodice together on F.L. Tack matching balance marks with R.S. together. Stitch.

FIG. 80

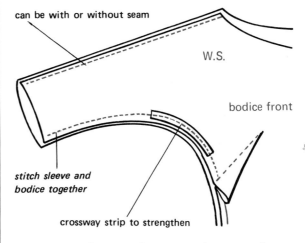

6. Remove tacking, and neaten edges according to fabric. Press open.

3. CAPE SLEEVE

This sleeve can be cut on S. of G. or crossway; it is inserted as for a plain sleeve.

FIG. 81

4. BISHOP SLEEVE

This sleeve is inserted as for a plain sleeve, apart from evenly adjusting the gathers.

FIG. 82

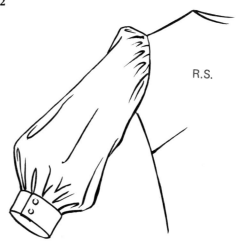

5. PUFF SLEEVE

As bishop sleeve.

FIG. 83

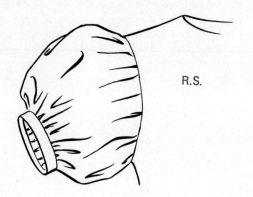

R.S.

6. CAP SLEEVE

As dolman sleeve.

FIG. 84

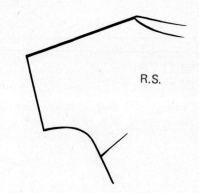

R.S.

Chapter 15

DISPOSAL OF FULLNESS

1. DARTS
2. TUCKS
3. GATHERS
4. EASING
5. SHIRRING
6. PLEATS
7. SMOCKING

1. DARTS

A. Dart Point One End

Method

1. Mark the darts through paper pattern and fabric. Remove pattern and cut through tailor's tacks.
2. Fold and pin the dart, so tailor's tacks meet together R.S. to R.S. Tack along the marked position on the W.S.

FIG. 85(a)

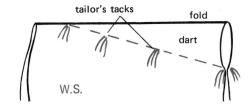

3. Remove tailor's tacks and machine stitch over tacking. The last three stitches at the point should lie right on the fold edge. Work from the wide end to the point.

FIG. 85(b)

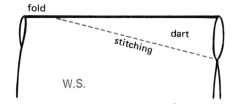

4. Neaten thread ends, tie at wide end and darn in at point.
5. Remove tacking and press dart flat to one side, unless dart is very wide or fabric thick: it must then be cut, neatened and pressed open.

FIG. 85(c)

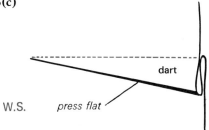

Uses

A functional dart, for shaping at bust, waist, neck and sleeve underside elbow.

B. Dart Point Each End

Method

1. Tack and stitch as previous dart, with great care to stitch close to the fold at points.

FIG. 86(a)

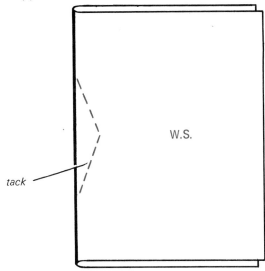

47

2. If this dart is deep, it will require clipping in the centre, cutting open and neatening. Press accordingly.

FIG. 86(b)

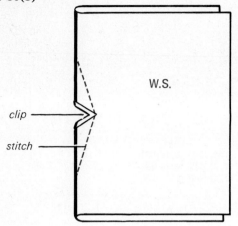

FIG. 86(c)

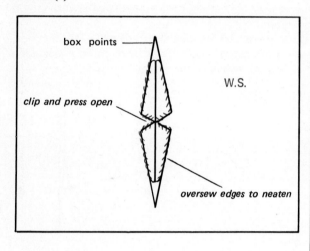

2. TUCKS

Tucks of 2 mm or less are called pin tucks, and are not pressed flat. Tucks over this size are pressed flat to one side. Tucks are more satisfactory on fine fabric.

Method

1. Mark each tuck position to allow for the width of the fold and the space between tucks.

FIG. 87(a)

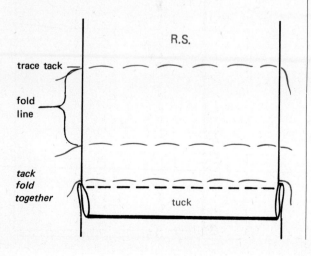

2. The fold edge is best marked with trace tacks. When machine stitching the tucks a special attachment can be used.
3. Pin and tack along the fold of each tuck on the R.S.
4. Machine stitch or do hand running stitch along each tacking line, through two thicknesses of the fold, on the R.S.

FIG. 87(b)

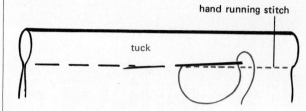

5. Press tucks flat into position.

FIG. 87(c)

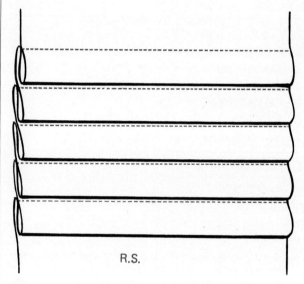

Uses

To dispose of fullness, or as a decoration on bodices, yokes, cuffs, hems of children's clothes to lengthen by unpicking a tuck as required.

3. GATHERS

Method

1. Work two rows of fine running stitch, along the F.L. and 0.5 cm above. Start with a firm stitch, and leave end threads free.

FIG. 88(a)

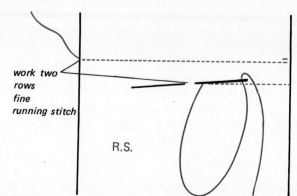

2. The two rows of thread are drawn up together evenly to the required length, then wound round a pin. The resulting gathers may then be evenly distributed.

FIG. 88(b)

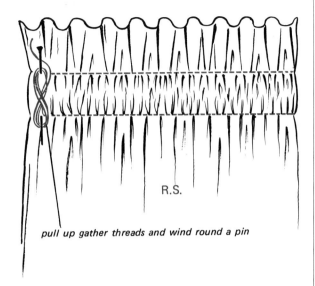

pull up gather threads and wind round a pin

Uses
Gathers in puff sleeves, skirt waists, yokes, etc.

4. EASING
Method

The same preparation as gathering, but the threads are only drawn up very slightly, to give a small amount of fullness with no pleating, e.g. sleeve head.

5. SHIRRING
Method

Work as for gathering doing three or more rows, which are then pulled up evenly. Used mainly as a decoration.

FIG. 89

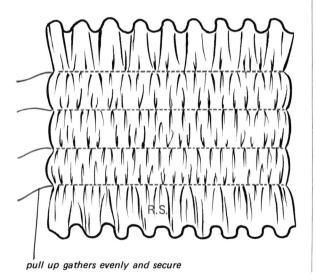

pull up gathers evenly and secure

6. PLEATS
A. Knife Pleats
B. Inverted Pleats
C. Box Pleats
D. Backed Inverted Pleat
E. Concertina Pleats
F. Sunray Pleats

Note: A pleat is formed by a fold of fabric forming three layers.

A. Knife Pleats
A series of folds facing in the same direction.

Method

1. Mark pleat lines with two colours.

FIG. 90(a)

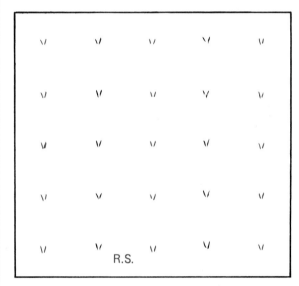

2. Bring one colour mark over to the other and pin into position from top to bottom, through three thicknesses of fabric. Tack.
3. Repeat the above process until all pleats are tacked; then press lightly.

FIG. 90(b)

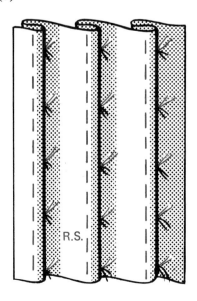

B. Inverted Pleats
Method

Work in the same way as knife pleats, but bring two folds together so that they meet.

FIG. 91

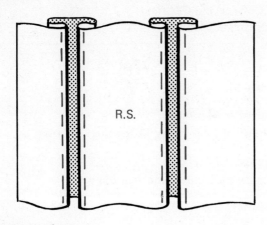

C. Box Pleats
Method

Work as for knife pleats, but turn two folds away from each other.

FIG. 92

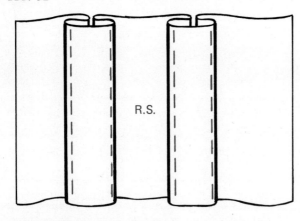

D. Backed Inverted Pleat
Method

1. Tack and press back the pleat folds equally on sections 1 and 2. Place folds flat so they meet in the centre, W.S. garment uppermost.

FIG. 93(a)

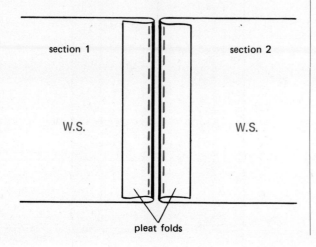

2. Cut a backing strip to cover the two pleat folds, tack into position and stitch as diagram shows.

FIG. 93(b)

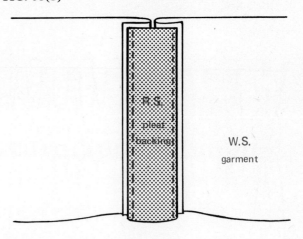

3. Remove tacking and press.

FIG. 93(c)

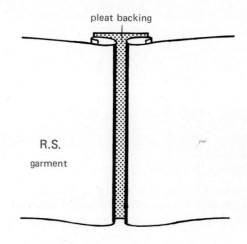

E. Concertina Pleats

These are as their name implies; they must not be deeper than 1.25 cm because they do not lie flat.

Method

These pleats should be done commercially by a permanent press process.

FIG. 94

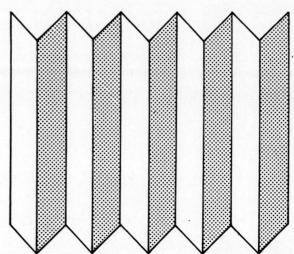

F. Sunray Pleats

Method

Fabric is cut circular or semi-circular, then pleated permanently, commercially.

FIG. 95(a)

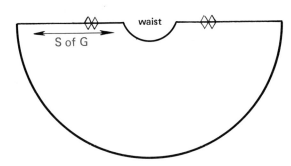

FIG. 95(b)

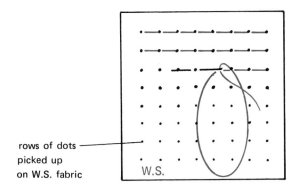

Uses

Mostly for skirts or trimmings.

7. SMOCKING

Preparation

Method

1. If check material is used no marking is required, as the check lines can be used as a guide.
2. When using plain fabric a sheet of transfer dots can be used.
3. With W.S. fabric uppermost, place your transfer in position, shiny side to fabric. Pin the transfer to the fabric at outer edges.
4. Press the transfer onto the fabric with a fairly warm iron. Check that the transfer has 'taken', then peel off the paper.
5. Using a contrasting colour of thread pick up the dots in rows across the fabric from right to left on the W.S. starting with a very secure stitch, and leaving the other end free. Do not pull up until all rows are completed.

FIG. 96(a)

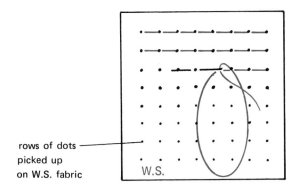

rows of dots
picked up
on W.S. fabric

6. Draw up two sets of threads at a time, to a third of the original size. Wind threads round a pin.

FIG. 96(b)

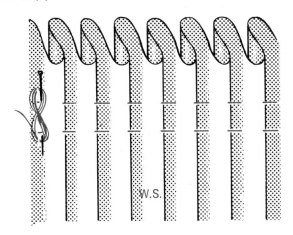

Basic Smocking Stitches

Method as Diagram

A. **Outline stitch**—worked left to right with the thread below or above the needle but always in the same direction each stitch.
B. **Cable stitch**—worked left to right one stitch to each pleat, with the thread alternately above and below the needle.
C. **Wave stitch**—worked left to right as a variation of B.
D. **Diamond stitch**—worked left to right. The top stitch is worked with the thread above the needle, the stitch then passes diagonally on to the next pleat and is worked with the thread below.

Many other basic embroidery stitches can be used in smocking.

FIG. 97

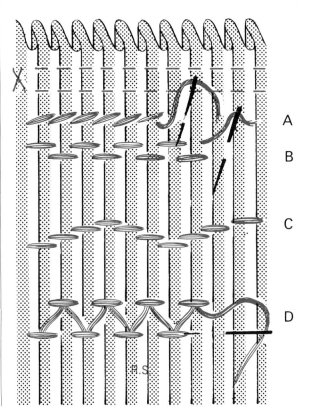

Chapter 16

POCKETS

1. PATCH POCKETS
2. POCKET IN A SEAM
3. BOUND POCKETS

1. PATCH POCKETS

A. Pointed Bottom with Shaped Facing

Method

1. Turn under the shaped edge of facing to W.S. on P.L., cut away bulk of turnings at the point, tack edge and press.

FIG. 98(a)

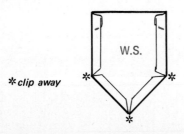

2. Pin and tack the facing to pocket top, R.S. facing to W.S. pocket; stitch, remove tacking and trim turnings to 0.5 cm. Press facing over to R.S. of pocket and press flat then machine stitch to the pocket.
3. Turn sides and bottom of pocket over to W.S. on P.L.; cut away bulk at corners, tack edge of folded turnings and press.
4. Pin, tack and stitch pocket to garment, remove tacking and press.

FIG. 98(b)

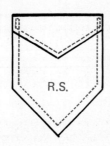

B. Square with Self Hem on R.S.

As for A., with the exception of the top, which is a self hem finished on the W.S. with top stitching.

FIG. 99(a)   **FIG. 99(b)**

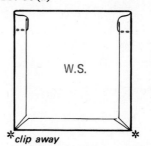 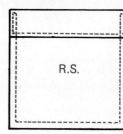

C. Round Corners with Self Hem on W.S.

Method

1. Finish a hem on the W.S. top.
2. Turn remaining edges over to the W.S. on P.L., tacking this edge near the fold. Clip away surplus bulk at corners.

FIG. 100(a)   **FIG. 100(b)**

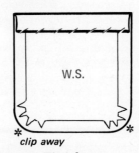 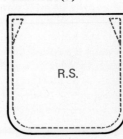

Corner Finishes.

FIG. 101   **FIG. 102**

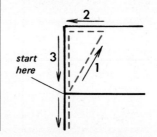 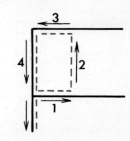

2. POCKET IN A SEAM

Method

1. Pin and tack the pocket pieces to garment back and front respectively, R.S. to R.S., matching balance marks.
2. Machine on the pattern line leaving seam allowance at top and bottom free. Remove tacking.

FIG. 103(a)

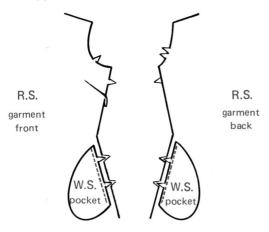

3. Complete the garment side seams above and below the pocket and press seam open.

FIG. 103(b)

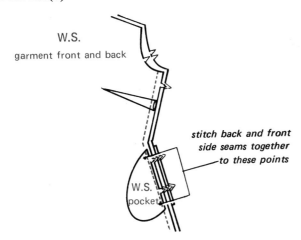

4. Pin, tack and machine pocket together R.S. to R.S., being sure the start and finish of this stitching meets the side seam stitching.
5. Neaten edges and press pocket towards garment front.

FIG. 103(c)

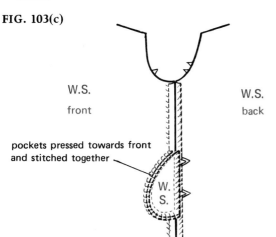

3. BOUND POCKET

(The first stage is the same method as a bound buttonhole.)

Method

1. Mark the pocket's exact position on the garment with a line of tacking.

FIG. 104(a)

2. The material to form the bind and pocket is cut in one strip, i.e. for a pocket 11 cm long and 13 cm deep, cut a strip 15 cm wide by 30 cm long, on S. of G.
3. Pin the strip R.S. to R.S. on the garment evenly over the tack mark but with more than half the strip above the tack mark, and tack firmly.

FIG. 104(b)

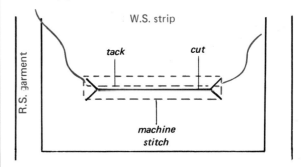

4. Stitch the strip to the garment on the W.S. 0.5 cm each side of the tack mark to form a rectangle. Cut and bind the slit as for a bound buttonhole. Press and tack bind together.

FIG. 104(c)

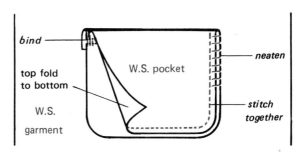

5. On the W.S. fold the pocket top down to cover the bottom, and stitch together with rounded corners; trim and level edges, neaten and press.

FIG. 104(d)

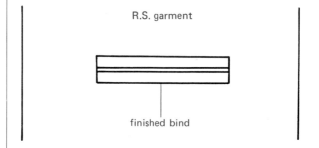

Note: great care should be taken not to stretch the work when the fabric has been cut on the cross-grain.

Chapter 17

HEMS

1. LEVELLING A HEM
2. TURNING UP A SKIRT HEM
3. HEM METHODS AND
   NEATENINGS

1. LEVELLING A HEM
A. On a Figure

Method
1. If the hem is shaped it should be allowed to hang for some time.
2. The wearer should stand on a table, and the fitter will then mark the desired hem line with pins or chalk, using a yardstick or hem measure, and measuring upwards from the table.

B. Flat

Method
Fold the garment in half quite flat and level on a table, then measure from the waist down and mark all round with pins or chalk.

FIG. 106

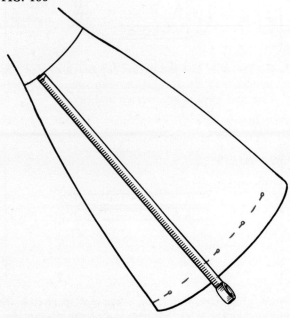

FIG. 105

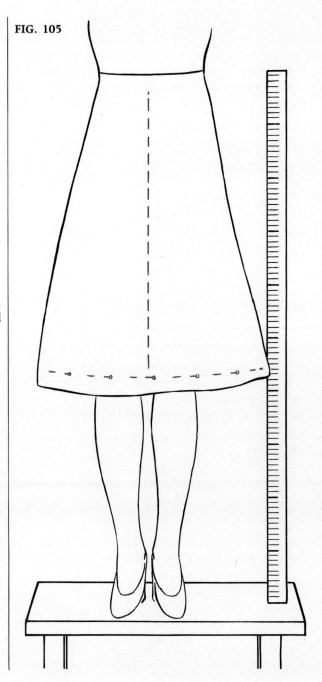

54

2. TURNING UP A SKIRT HEM

Note: The fuller the skirt, the narrower the hem.

Method

1. With the hem facing towards you flat on a table, fold the turning over to the W.S. on the marked line. Pin, then tack 2 cm from the fold all round the hem.
2. With hem still flat on the table, measure from the fold edge the required width and mark with chalk. Cut away the surplus fabric and complete this edge according to the fabric and hem width as in figures below.

3. HEM METHODS AND NEATENINGS

A. Narrow Shaped Hem

Method

Tack, press and slip stitch hem, remove tacking and press.

FIG. 107

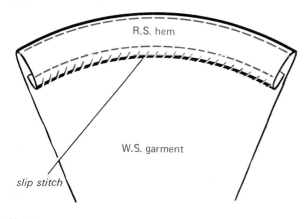

Uses

On full flared skirts.

B. Wider Shaped Hem

Method

Pleat, pin and tack hem evenly. Turn edge under, slip stitch and press.

FIG. 108

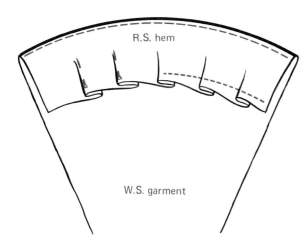

Uses

Where a deeper hem is desirable.

C. Wide Hem, Soft Fabric

Method

Run gather thread along free edge and draw up to fit the garment, then shrink fabric with an iron and damp cloth on W.S. Finish edge according to fabric.

FIG. 109

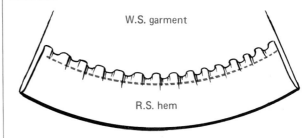

D. Herringboned Hem

Method

Prepare hem with one turning then herringbone stitch down.

FIG. 110

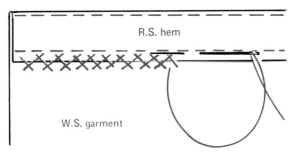

Uses

On jersey and velvet.

E. Very Narrow Hem

(Machine stitched)

Method

1. Turn hem over once 0.5 cm and machine very near the fold. Trim close to stitching.

FIG. 111(a)

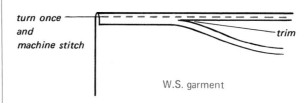

2. Turn hem over once again as narrowly as possible and machine again.

FIG. 111(b)

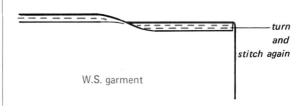

Uses

Dainty fabrics. Ideal when attaching lace, and also edging frills.

F. Bound Hem (flat)

Use Paris or Prussian binding (which has a twill weave) or tape.

Method

Pin, tack and stitch the bind along the prepared hem edge, then slip stitch, press and remove tacks. This edge can also be found with a crosscut strip; it must then be treated as an edge binding and turned under to neaten.

FIG. 112

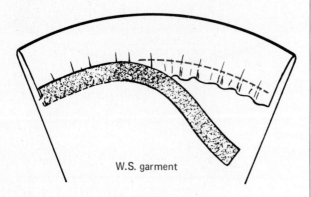

W.S. garment

Uses

For fabrics that fray easily.

G. Hem with Edge Stitched Turning
Method

Turn under free edge and machine along the folded edge. Press and tack into position, then slip stitch and press.

FIG. 113

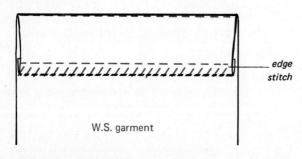

edge stitch

W.S. garment

Uses

For non-iron and springy fabrics.

H. Faced Hem
Method

1. Cut a piece of self fabric, on S. of G. for a straight hem and on cross grain for a shaped hem. Pin, tack and stitch the strip R.S. to R.S. along the edge to be faced.

FIG. 114

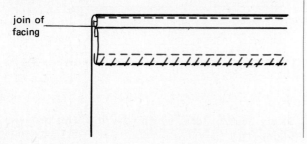

join of facing

2. Remove the tacking and press the seam open, then slightly over to the garment W.S. to form a false hem; complete the hem and press.

Uses

To lengthen garments and finish shaped edges.

I. To Mitre a Corner on a Plain Hem
Method

1. Mark in the hem position on both edges equally.

FIG. 115(a)

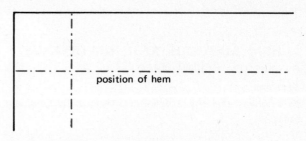

position of hem

2. Fold corner to point where marked lines cross and cut on fold.

FIG. 115(b)

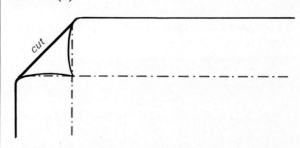

cut

3. Fold this edge so that line of fold passes through point where marked lines cross. Make narrow turnings on other two raw edges. (Fig. 115c and d)

FIG. 115(c)   **FIG. 115(d)**

turn

fold here

turn   fold here

4. Bring the two corners together, folding along the marked lines. This forms the mitre. This corner seam may be neatly oversewn.

FIG. 115(e)

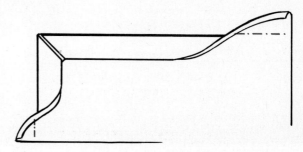

Chapter 18

WAISTBANDS AND BELTS

1. SOFT OR STIFFENED WAISTBANDS
2. PETERSHAM WAIST FINISH
3. UNSTIFFENED BELTS
4. STIFFENED BELTS

1. SOFT OR STIFFENED WAISTBANDS.
Method

1. Mark in the fold line of band centre.
2. Using interfacing or tailor's canvas, bonded interfacing or petersham, cut to the exact width and length of the finished band; tack then machine to the band back on W.S.

FIG. 116(a)

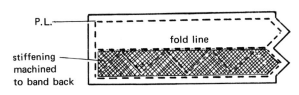

3. Fold band in half along fold line with W.S. outside. Stitch and trim each end as diagram shows.

FIG. 116(b)

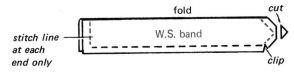

4. Turn band to R.S. and press.

FIG. 116(c)

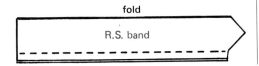

5. Pin then tack R.S. front band section to skirt waist with pointed end at overlap.

FIG. 116(d)

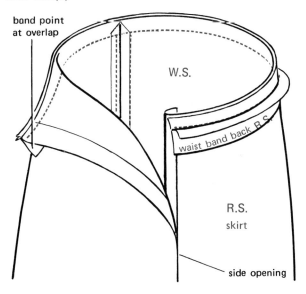

6. Trim turnings then pull the band upwards and fold the free edge over the turnings, tack and hem firmly on the pattern line. Press.

FIG. 116(e)

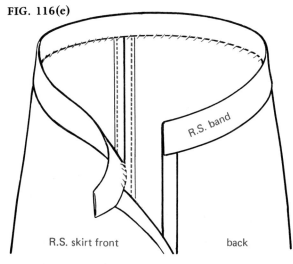

2. PETERSHAM WAIST FINISH
Method

1. Take a length of skirt waist petersham: waist size plus wrap and 1 cm turnings each end; also a matching length of paris binding.
2. Stitch the binding to the petersham so that it is level with the edge and leaving space for the skirt waist edge to be inserted.
3. Insert the skirt waist round edge between the petersham and the bind, covering the raw edge and neatly turning in both edges. Tack and machine through all thicknesses.

FIG. 117(a)

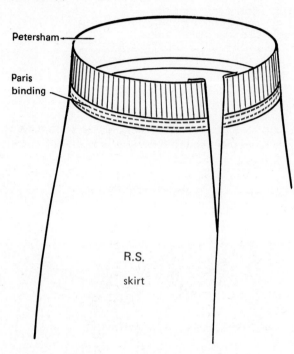

4. Remove tacking and press the whole over to the skirt W.S. Neaten ends and complete the side opening (or placket) with fastenings.

FIG. 117(b)

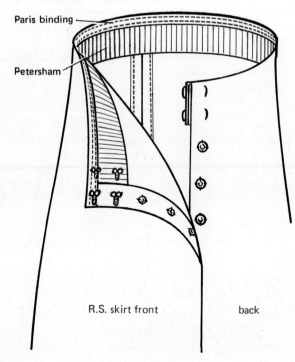

3. UNSTIFFENED BELTS
Method

1. Cut a strip of fabric twice the finished width plus turnings and the length of the waist size plus 8 cm for wrap.
2. Fold the strip in half lengthwise, W.S. out. Tack and stitch round three sides leaving the centre unstitched for turning through as diagram shows.

FIG. 118(a)

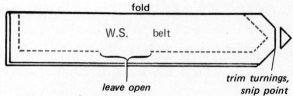

3. Trim turnings, snip corners, turn belt to R.S. Slip stitch opening together and press.

FIG. 118(b)

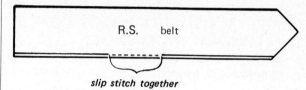

4. STIFFENED BELTS
Method

1. Cut a strip of fabric on S.G. as for unstiffened belt, plus a strip of interfacing the size of the finished belt.
2. Mark the centre lengthwise, fold with a pressed crease and baste the interfacing along this fold on W.S.

FIG. 119(a)

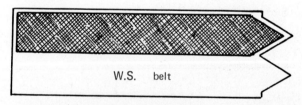

3. Fold all the turnings to the W.S. exactly on the pattern line, mitreing the corners.

FIG. 119(b)

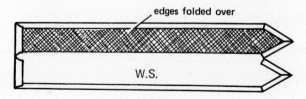

4. Fold edges together and tack on R.S. all round.
5. Machine all round the edge; to complete add eyelet holes and buckle, press.

FIG. 119(c)

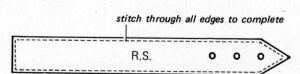

Chapter 19

LINGERIE

FABRICS, TRIMMINGS, SEAMS

Few people make underwear today, as unlike outer-wear it is better, stronger and cheaper when mass produced. This is owing to the use of special machines for stitching and neatening on difficult and fine fabrics and trimmings. However, nightwear, housecoats and petticoats for special occasions are well worth while making.

Fabrics. Tricot stretches and is therefore most comfortable for panties and slips, in nylon, tricel and polyesters. Woven fabrics are pure silk, rayon, cotton lawn, polyester and cotton blend. They must be fine, washable and shrinkproof, and also colour fast.

Trimmings should match the fabrics used as nearly as possible, but nylon lace and ribbon are used most often as nylon wears and washes best.

Seams must be fine and flat; those mostly used are:
Run and fell,
Double stitched,
French,
Plain seam, trimmed and neatened together.

USE OF LACE
Edgings

Nylon lace creases least; coarse cotton lace holds its shape. The rough side of lace is the R.S. There is usually a draw string thread along the straight edge of the lace that can be pulled up for gathering, attaching lace by hand to a hem with satin stitch, etc.

Method
1. Tack lace along neatened edge with small stitches.
2. Oversew with close fine satin stitch using a fine embroidery thread.
3. Cut away material at the back if no neatening is required, i.e. on non-fray fabrics.

FIG. 120

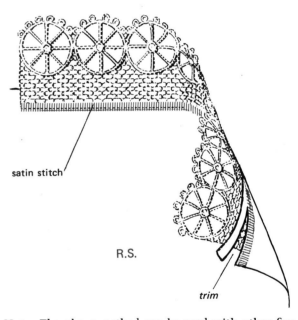

satin stitch

R.S.

trim

Note: The above method can be used with other firm embroidery stitches such as loop stitch, buttonhole stitch, etc., also machine zig-zag and embroidery.
The lace can be drawn up to form a frill and attached in the same way.

FIG. 121

draw string to frill lace

Joining Lace
Method
1. Place two exact lace motifs on top of each other with R.S. uppermost, and secure together with fine running stitches.
2. Oversew finely together all round the edge as diagram shows.

FIG. 122

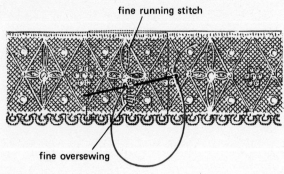

fine running stitch

fine oversewing

3. Cut away remaining lace outside the oversewing.

Shell Edging
Method
1. Press a hem edge about 1 cm wide.
2. Make two slip hem stitches then two tight oversew stitches pulling the thread tightly over the hem.
3. Continue evenly along the hem, forming scallops as you go. This is an attractive edge on fine fabrics.

FIG. 123

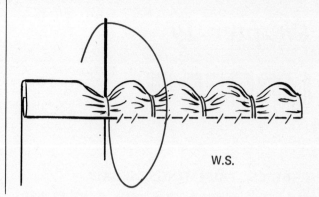

W.S.

Chapter 20

EMBROIDERY

---

1. EQUIPMENT, FABRIC AND THREADS

A. Basic Equipment
B. Fabrics
C. Threads

A. Basic Equipment

Needles: Embroidery, crewel, tapestry; fine to coarse. Threads.

Scissors: special sharp small embroidery scissors with fine points.

Tracing paper: various colours.

Transfers.

Pencil, ruler.

Note: Always use a fine needle and thread for fine fabric, and increase size according to fabric.

B. Fabrics Most Used

Cotton ⎤ These all wash well and can be in fine or coarse
Linen ⎬ weave according to the type of embroidery
Rayon ⎦ required.

C. Threads

Stranded cotton: (with a sheen) can be used 1–4 strands.

Cotton-a-broder: (with a sheen), unstranded, used on medium to heavy fabrics.

Cotton without a sheen: a thicker thread for coarse fabrics.

Pure silk: stranded for fine fabrics.

Tapestry wool: for canvas work.

2. BASIC EMBROIDERY STITCHES

A. Running Stitch

A simple evenly spaced stitch worked from right to left.

FIG. 124

B. Stem Stitch

An outline stitch, basic for smocking; worked from left to right.

FIG. 125

C. Back Stitch

Worked from right to left.

FIG. 126

D. Cross Stitch

Used greatly in canvas work. Worked from right to left, with threads counted, then left to right to form the cross.

FIG. 127

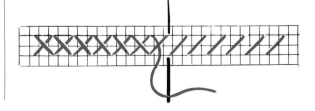

E. Herringbone Stitch

FIG. 128

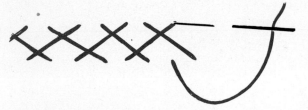

F. Chain Stitch

FIG. 129

G. Loop Stitch

Worked from left to right; also used to neaten edges.

FIG. 130

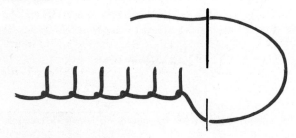

H. Buttonhole Stitch

Mostly worked over the edge of two thicknesses as for buttonholes. The knot lies at the edges and is formed in a figure of eight round the needle as diagram shows.

FIG. 131

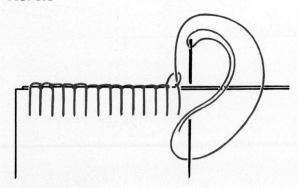

I. Satin Stitch

Worked over and over to fill in shape or to attach lace.

FIG. 132

J. Feather Stitch

Worked diagonally from left to right and right to left alternately.

FIG. 133

K. Couching

Another thread worked over two laid threads.

FIG. 134

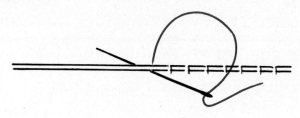

There can be many variations of basic stitches to form more advanced stitches once the basic stitches are mastered.

3. DESIGN

Transfers can be bought, these can be cut and arranged and your own designs added. Should you prefer to design your own work it can be done as follows:

Method A

1. Draw the design clearly on paper, trace off the design through tracing paper.
2. Place carbon paper between the tracing and fabric, then trace off the design.

Method B

Tack the traced design paper to the fabric, embroider over it, then tear the paper away.

4. APPLIQUÉ

This is a method of attaching one or many different fabrics over another to form a design, be it a collage picture or a dainty motif on fine fabric.

If the fabric does not fray (like felt) the designs can be drawn and cut out exactly, then applied. With other fabrics the design is drawn on the fabric to be applied, tacked to the underfabric, and the edge of the design is sewn closely round through all thicknesses, then cut closely away to the stitching.

Method

1. Draw design on fabric to be applied.
2. Work any embroidery lines on this fabric.
3. Baste the above fabric to the base.
4. Work fine running or oversewing round the edges of the design through the base.

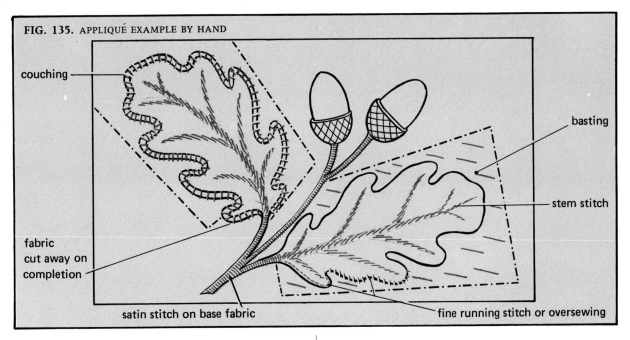

FIG. 135. APPLIQUÉ EXAMPLE BY HAND

couching

basting

stem stitch

fabric cut away on completion

satin stitch on base fabric

fine running stitch or oversewing

5. Work another firm decorative stitch over the previous edging.
6. Cut away surplus fabric round the edge, and press on the wrong side over a turkish towel

5. SHADOW EMBROIDERY

The designs for this must be narrow symmetrical motifs as they are to be filled in with close herringbone stitch on the wrong side forming an edging of back stitch on the right side, with the shadow of the herringbone showing through; so a fine fabric such as organdie,

lawn, fine silk is best, using a darker shade of silk.

Method

1. Choose or make a design as advised above.
2. Transfer the design to the fabric on the W.S.
3. With a suitable colour of fine embroidery thread, fill in the design with close herringbone stitch on the W.S., being sure that all ends are darned in invisibly.
4. When work is completed, press lightly on the worked side over a turkish towel.

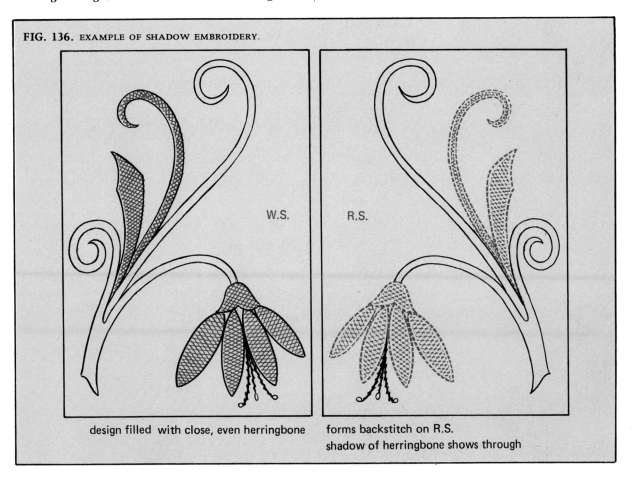

FIG. 136. EXAMPLE OF SHADOW EMBROIDERY.

W.S.

R.S.

design filled with close, even herringbone

forms backstitch on R.S.
shadow of herringbone shows through

6. QUILTING
A. Traditional Quilting
B. Italian Quilting

A. Traditional Quilting
This consists of three thicknesses of material, i.e. top fabric, a padding of wadding, soft cotton or flannel, and a lining.

Method
1. Place the three layers together quite flat, and baste through all thicknesses firmly.
2. The three thicknesses can then be stitched through by hand or machine.
   By hand: small running stitches through all thicknesses in a chosen design.

By machine: stitch in straight even lines to form squares or diamonds, using a special quilting attachment on the machine.
3. Remove tacking and use as required.

B. Italian Quilting
This is prepared in a way similar to that above, but the padding should not be too thick, and the bottom layer of fabric should be of loosely woven cotton. The structure of the design must form two lines of running stitch to outline each shape. (See Fig. 137.) When the design has been hand stitched, a soft thick cord of silk or cotton is threaded through a large-eyed blunt needle, and the back lining is pierced. The cord is threaded through the two lines of stitching between the lining and the padding, causing the pattern to rise in a cord on the R.S.

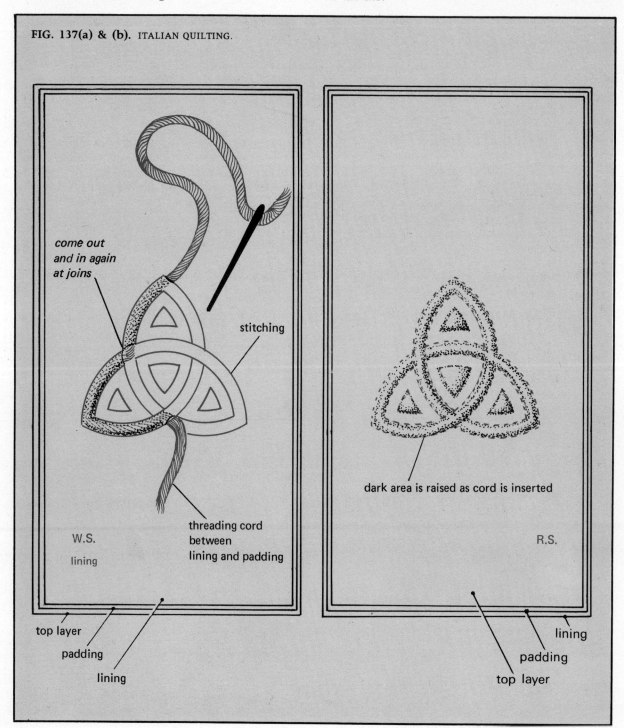

FIG. 137(a) & (b). ITALIAN QUILTING.

come out
and in again
at joins

stitching

threading cord
between
lining and padding

W.S.

lining

top layer

padding

lining

dark area is raised as cord is inserted

R.S.

lining

padding

top layer

Chapter 21

REPAIRS

1. PATCHING
2. DARNING
3. CARE AND RENOVATION
4. STAIN REMOVAL

1. PATCHING
A. Household Patch
B. Print Patch
C. Flannel or Wool Patch
D. Cloth Patch
E. Machined Patch
F. Machined Darn for Slit or Tear

A. Household Patch
Method
1. Cut a patch to the required size on S. of G. plus 0.5 cm for turnings all round.
2. Fold and press the turnings to R.S. on all four sides as diagram shows.

FIG. 138(a)

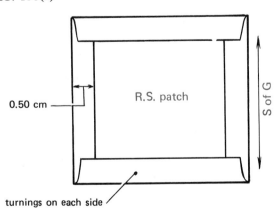

turnings on each side

3. Pin and tack the patch R.S. to W.S. garment over the holes and on S. of G.
4. Machine stitch or hem into position close to the fold.

FIG. 138(b)

patch pinned and tacked to garment

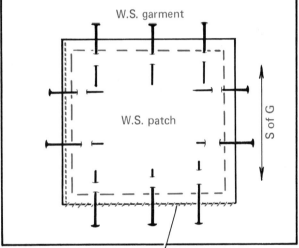

machined or hand hemmed down

5. Remove tacking, cut away worn part of fabric to within 1 cm from the stitching. Snip 0.5 cm into corners, and turn this edge under all round four sides. Tack and stitch down.

FIG. 138(c)

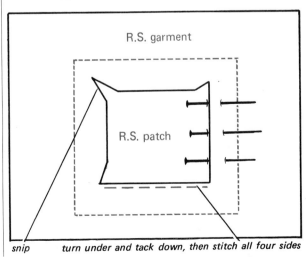

snip   turn under and tack down, then stitch all four sides

6. Completed patch.

FIG. 138(d)

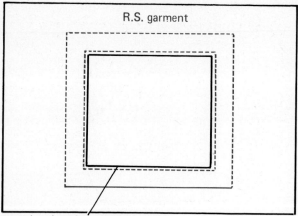

completed patch

R.S. garment

turned under edge stitched to patch

Uses

Where a strong patch is required, such as on bed linen, household linen, overalls, etc.

B. Print Patch
Method

1. Cut a patch to the required size on S. of G. and matching the pattern of the fabric to be repaired, plus 0.5 cm for turnings.
2. Fold and press the turnings over to the W.S.

FIG. 139(a)

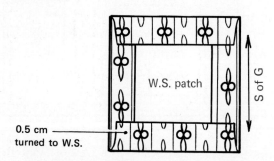

W.S. patch

S of G

0.5 cm turned to W.S.

3. Pin, tack and stitch the patch to the R.S., using stitching as invisible as possible.

FIG. 139(b)

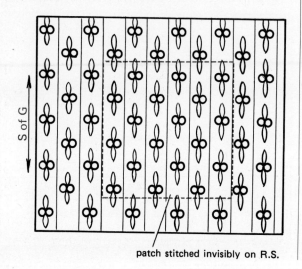

S of G

patch stitched invisibly on R.S.

4. On the W.S. cut away the hole to meet the edge of the patch turnings, and loop stitch these two edges together.

FIG. 139(c)

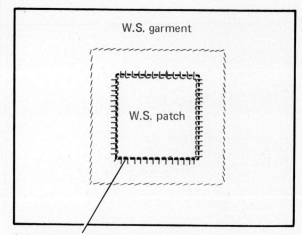

W.S. garment

W.S. patch

hole cut away and the two edges only loop stitched together

Uses

Where an invisible outer patch is required.

C. Flannel or Wool Patch
Method

1. Cut a patch to required size on S. of G. with no turnings, slightly rounding the corners.

FIG. 140(a)

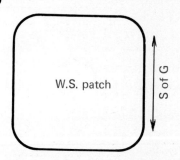

W.S. patch

S of G

2. Pin and tack the patch over the hole on S. of G., R.S. to W.S., garment.
3. Herringbone stitch the patch to the garment.

FIG. 140(b)

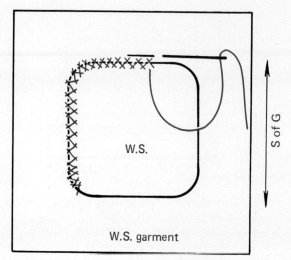

W.S.

S of G

W.S. garment

4. Cut away the worn fabric to 0.5 cm from the stitching with slightly rounded corners; herringbone stitch this edge to the patch and press.

FIG. 140(c)

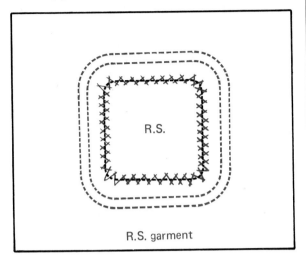

R.S.

R.S. garment

Uses

To repair fine wool and knitted underwear.

D. Cloth Patch
Method

1. Cut a patch on S. of G. to exact measurements of worn area, plus 1 cm turnings.

FIG. 141(a)

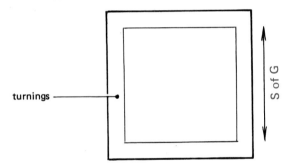

turnings

S of G

2. Mark the exact size of the patch evenly over the part to be mended on S. of G., with chalk or tacking. Cut away the worn or damaged part to within 1 cm of this mark and snip diagonally into the corners.

FIG. 141(b)

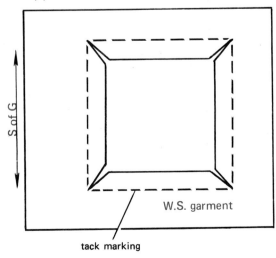

S of G

W.S. garment

tack marking

3. Place patch R.S. to W.S. garment over the worn area. Lift the garment prepared edges to fit the patch as diagram shows, and tack into position equally on all four sides, with special care at the corners.

FIG. 141(c)

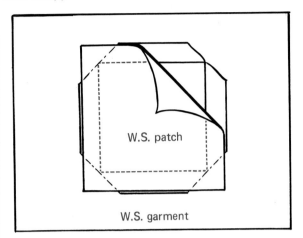

W.S. patch

W.S. garment

4. Back stitch or machine stitch the two edges together along the four sides.
5. Snip away the surplus fabric on the patch corners, then press seams open. Neaten all raw edges with loop stitch.

FIG. 141(d)

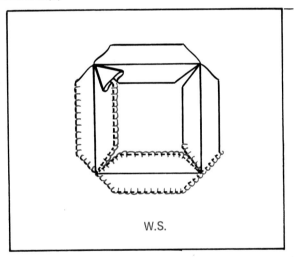

W.S.

FIG. 141(e)

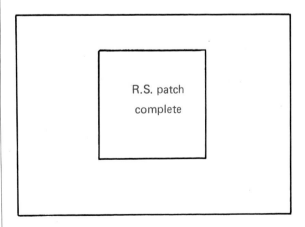

R.S. patch

complete

Uses

Where an inconspicuous repair on wool fabric is needed.

E. Machined Patch

Method

1. Cut a patch on S. of G. to the size required, with slightly rounded corners.
2. Tack patch into position on S. of G., R.S. patch to W.S. article, without turnings.
3. Machine zig-zag closely over raw edge of patch onto the article. Remove tacking.

FIG. 142(a)

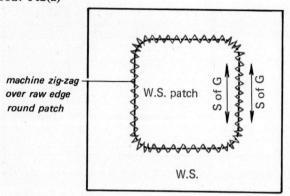

4. Turn over to R.S. and cut away worn part to 1 cm from stitching line. Tack, then machine zig-zag down this edge. Remove tacking and press.

FIG. 142(b)

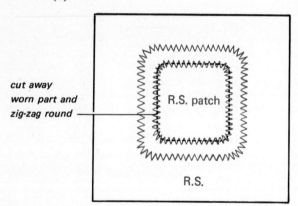

Uses

For under garments of stretch fabric, and household linens.

F. Machine Mending a Slit or Tear
Method

1. Draw together the slit with fishbone stitch by hand.

FIG. 143(a)

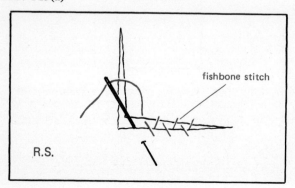

2. Cut a strip of fabric to cover the slit, and tack this over it on the W.S.

FIG. 143(b)

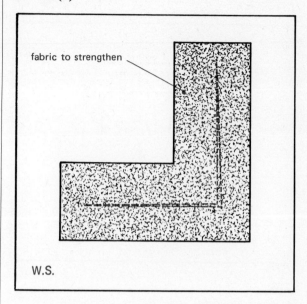

3. Place the work in an embroidery frame, R.S. up. Set the machine for darning by dropping the feed dog.
4. Stitch the darn by moving the frame manually backwards and forwards over the slit until it is covered. Remove tacking and press.

FIG. 143(c)

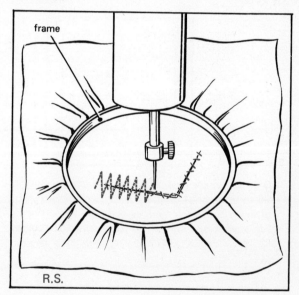

Uses

Household linens, overalls, etc.

2. DARNING
A. Stocking Darn
B. Hedgetear Darn

A. Stocking Darn
Method

1. Place the hole to be darned over a darning mushroom or ball, to prevent the threads from drawing together.

FIG. 144

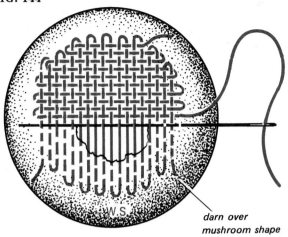

darn over
mushroom shape

2. Using fine matching wool or thread and a darning needle, weave first in one direction, picking up all free loops round the hole; and then in the opposite direction until the hole and its surround are covered. Leave loops at each turn of thread to allow for shrinkage.

B. Hedgetear Darn
Method

1. Draw edges together with fishbone stitch on W.S.
2. Darn over area of slit starting 1 cm from the end, and continuing to 1 cm past the corner. Cut thread.

FIG. 145(a)

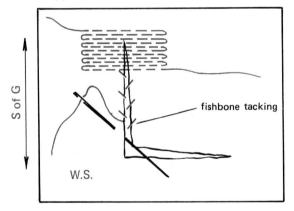

fishbone tacking

S of G

W.S.

3. Turn work round in order to double-darn the corner, then continue to 1 cm past the remaining point.

FIG. 145(b)

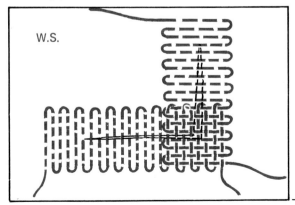

W.S.

Used on straight cuts only.

3. CARE OF CLOTHES
A. Cleaning and Washing
B. Storing
C. General Repairs

A. Cleaning and Washing

Cleaning garments can be done by a reputable commercial firm if they must not be laundered; a guide to this should always be ascertained when the garment is bought. Most garments today have a symbol chart on the label to guide you, such as the one below.

FIG. 146

washing instructions and programme number

	MACHINE	HAND WASH
6	WARM (40°C) MINIMUM WASH	WARM (40°C)
	COLD RINSE	DO NOT WRING

do not iron   **A** dry cleanable

alternative

P   ⊗

dry clean   *do not bleach*

It is wise to point out these instructions to cleaners, also what the fabric is made from and any indication of colour fastness, drip dry, proofing against rain or moth or permanent press. Laundering should be done frequently according to the fabric. Much research has been done by most manufacturers and consumer councils, so follow their advice with care. Garments that are stored when soiled attract moths and mildew and are not ready to wear when required. Fabrics last much longer if grime and body acids are not left in to weaken and rot the fibres.

B. Storing Clothes

Coats

These should be hung on a good hanger, and buttoned up to keep their shape.

Suits

Treat these as coats, but using a special skirt hanger, or one with hooks for skirt loops.

Slacks

Hang with their creases level, over the bar of a hanger.

Blouses

Hang these, if not crease-resistant, otherwise fold them neatly into a drawer.

Shoes

A special shoe cupboard with fitted rungs is ideal; otherwise plastic shoe hangers with pockets are available. Store light dress and evening shoes in plastic bags.

Stockings, Tights, Socks

These should all be clean, mended and stored in pairs in sorted plastic bags.

Underwear

This should be sorted into kinds, mended, cleaned and folded neatly.

Sun and Swimwear

This should be clean and kept in plastic bags.

Sweaters

Clean sweaters should be folded into sealed plastic bags to keep out moths.

Accessories

Bags, scarves, belts, jewellery, etc.
Use shelves or drawers that make selection easy.

C. General Repairs

Do these frequently. Mend loops, straps, elastic, linings, seams, holes, buttons, etc. 'A stitch in time saves nine.'

Renovations

Many favourite garments can be altered, improved and made fashionable with a little initiative. Lengths can always be brought up to date by adjusting hems, shorter or longer; necklines may be cut out, faced or bound; collars and cuffs, smart pockets, belts and trimmings added. Otherwise garments can be unpicked, washed, pressed and remade.

4. STAIN REMOVAL

Candlewax: scrape off, put blotting paper over and under fabric, then apply a hot iron.

Chewing Gum: scrape off, then rub with carbon tetrachloride.

Coffee and Cocoa: launder, or clean with wood alcohol.

Milk, Cream and Butter: soak in clear water, then launder.

Egg: launder, or use hydrogen peroxide to clean.

Glue: clean with equal parts of vinegar and water.

Grass: launder using a small amount of bleach.

Grease and Oil: rub off excess; rub lard into tar, then launder; otherwise use carbon tetrachloride.

Ink: launder if the ink is the washable variety; otherwise soak in milk for two days, then launder.

Rust: remove with an equal mixture of salt and lemon juice, then launder.

Lipstick: use carbon tetrachloride or hydrogen peroxide, if this is suitable for the fabric.

Mildew: soak in sour milk for some time, then launder.

Nail Varnish: sponge with acetone, then launder.

Paint: rub with turpentine, then launder.

Blood: soak in cold water, then launder.

Note: Where articles are not launderable sponge the area gently over a thick towel, using tepid water, then blot and leave to dry. When removing stains, use a soft colourless cloth, soak it in the liquid to be used and spread the liquid lightly outwards to avoid making a ring. Work on the wrong side first over a towel, then lightly on the right side.

Sponging and Pressing

1. Brush the garment well all over.
2. Rub lightly all over with a damp clean cloth.
3. Treat any stains.
4. Turn to the wrong side and press over a soft cloth and with a damp cloth.
5. To remove shine, press on the R.S. with a wet cloth. Hold the iron 1 cm from the surface to create steam.

INDEX